Sacramental Ministry to a Diverse Generation

Sacramental Ministry to a Diverse Generation

Margaret L. Black

Sheed & Ward
Kansas City

Sheed & Ward™ is a service of The National Catholic
Reporter Publishing Company.

Library of Congress Cataloguing-in-Publication Data
Black, Margaret L., 1951-
        Sacramental ministry to a diverse generation
/ by Margaret L. Black.
                p.   cm.
        Originally presented as the author's thesis
(master's)—Xavier University.
        Includes bibliographical references.
        ISBN: 1-55612-976-9 (alk. paper)
        1. Church work with the baby boom generation.
2. Pastoral theology—Catholic Church.
3. Sacraments—Catholic Church. 4. Catholic Church—
Doctrines. 5. Catholic Church—United States—
Membership. I. Title.
        BX2347.8.B32B57 1997
        259'.08'4—dc21   97-20331
                                                    CIP

Published by: Sheed & Ward
                115 E. Armour Blvd.
                P.O. Box 419492
                Kansas City, MO 64141-6492

To order, call: (800) 333-7373

www.natcath.com/sheedward

Cover illustration and design by James F. Brisson.

To Jack, Craig and Jeff who taught me more about sacrament than any book I've read or workshop I've attended. To paraphrase a current song, I'm everything I am because you love me.

Contents

Acknowledgments

This book began as a project for my master's thesis at Xavier University. As it evolved, my advisor, Brennan Hill encouraged me to further develop it and submit it to be published. Throughout discussions with my colleagues in CREA (Cincinnati Religious Educators Association) I received support and affirmation. In fact, Donna Glaser nominated my work for an award from the National Conference of Catechetical Leadership. She said she did it for two reasons: one because she felt it deserved an award and secondly, to give me the push I needed to submit it to a publisher. Thanks Brennan, CREA members and Donna!

I would also like to thank Barry Mersmann, Marge Blessing, and especially Sister Marie Re, S.C. who provided much guidance in my ministry to Baby Boomers. Your assistance helped me glean wisdom from the chaos.

To Janie Reinart whose creative genius nudged mine into gear as we worked on parallel learning models for children in sacramental preparation and parish mission. Many of the ideas we used are incorporated in the Family Focused Preparation.

In addition to Dr. Hill, I am grateful to my professors at Xavier University for challenging me to

expand my own sacramental and theological understandings.

Thanks to all who ministered with me and to me,
listing all your names would make this section longer
than the book. Please know that I give thanks for
your guidance and friendship.

And, to my parents: you were truly my first Religious Education models; you wrote in my prayer
book, "May your faith always be as strong as our love
for you," I believe it is.

Preface

I am a Baby Boomer. I am a convert to the Roman Catholic religion. I am currently serving as a Family Life Minister having served for 14 years as a Parish Director of Religious Education. I have ministered in a small rural parish, a medium sized inner city community and most recently in a large suburban parish. Parishes today are inundated with Baby Boomers who bring their children to the Church to participate in the sacraments. They are a diverse group, these adult faithful. Some are much younger than I, some older. Some are "cradle Catholics," some converts, and some are supportive, non-Catholic parents. Their theological understanding varies from liberal to conservative, from followers of Matthew Fox to followers of Bishop LeFebre. In one breath they ask how we can better educate (indoctrinate) the 8th grade confirmation class and lower the age limit so they don't have to continue to fight with them to go to religion classes.

Like my peers, I find this part of my job the most rewarding and the most confrontational and often the most disheartening. It is the part I love and hate the most.

The Baby Boomer generation has been confronting and confounding at every stage of its growth. As they reach midlife and return to organized religion, the Boomer impact will alter the religious landscape. I have come to the conclusion that if I am to effectively minister to my own generation and to survive as a minister of the Church, then I must explore some crucial questions: What is it about the sacraments that anchored the Catholic Baby Boomer, caused them to defect, and brought them back? Why is there such a diverse understanding/interpretation of the sacraments within this generation? What type of paradigm shift will be needed to sacramentally minister to the Baby Boomers?

In order to answer these questions I have researched the Baby Boomer generation from a statistical viewpoint, a sociological understanding, and a psychological interpretation. I have read volumes of books and articles on "them." I have interviewed Baby Boomers and people who minister to them. I have shared in-depth conversations with their ministers, religious educators and evaluators. I have reread books and articles on Sacraments. Indeed, I have renewed my own sacramental imagination and found that over my course of study it has shifted a great deal.

Thus, *Sacramental Ministry to a Diverse Generation* is a culmination of my research, work and experience as a student of theology and humankind, director of religious education and a Catholic Baby Boomer. It is my reaction to the Baby Boomer challenge. How well I have met this challenge will be determined by the reader's reaction and the response from those to whom and with whom I minister.

Introduction

National statistics indicate that 83 to 86% of Baby
Boomers who grew up Catholic still identify themselves as Catholics, compared to 65% of mainline
Protestants and 80% of conservative Protestants. As
religious educators, ministers and theologians, it is
important to determine why more Catholics than Protestants still identify themselves with the religion of
their parents. An exploration of the sacramental principle demonstrates that it is the Baby Boomers' Sacramentality which has grounded their faith, given
them stability, at times caused them to defect, after
a responsible search brought them back, and today
is causing religious educators who are serving them
to have new insights into religious formation.

In order to adequately research the subject of
Baby Boomers and their sacramental perspective, I
utilized a four-step process. First, I reviewed my own
experience both as a parish director of religious education and a Baby Boomer and became a more active
listener in ministering with Baby Boomers. Secondly,
I did extensive research by reading specific Baby
Boomer-oriented materials regarding their cultural,
psychological, and spiritual profiles. I read and reread
books and periodicals on the sacraments, Church

and evangelization. Third, I interviewed Baby Boomers (Loyalists, Returnees and Dropouts), other directors of religious education, archdiocesan personnel, theologians, the Director of the Lay Pastoral Ministry Program in the Archdiocese of Cincinnati, and Baby Boomer priests. Finally, I attempted to process and transcribe the volumes of knowledge and useful insights I gained into a readable work, entitled *Sacramental Ministry to a Diverse Generation.*

Chapter 1, *Defining the Baby Boomer Generation*, provides the reader with a working understanding of the Baby Boomer generation. Never before has a generation been more inaccurately labeled or judged so harshly. Sociologists and psychologists continually point out that if one is to understand this generation, one must be aware of the cultural events experienced during their adolescence and early adulthood. The turbulence of the 1960s had a profound effect on this generation and changed the shape of the world for generations to come. The Vietnam War, rock and roll, drugs and Vatican II are a part of that chaotic period. The birthrate over the eighteen-year span (1946-1964) can be divided into two waves. These two waves are separated not just by years but by cultural experiences as well. For Catholic Baby Boomers, the two waves are further delineated by the occurrence and outcomes of Vatican II. Baby Boomers are grouped into four specific economic/vocational categories. Their lifestyles are explored, especially in their relationship to formalized religion. This section culminates with a look at Baby Boomers' relationship with the Catholic Church.

Chapter 2, *Range of Sacramental Understanding among Catholics*, identifies the sacraments as rites, rituals, community and celebrations. The nature of sacrament is presented. Andrew Greeley cites a significant difference between Catholics and Protestants in their understanding of sacrament. It is not just in identifying what is a sacrament but the depth of their sacramental perception that is "Sacramental Imagination." While Greeley defines this as the viewing of all creation as a sacrament, this theological explanation is beyond the comprehension of the average person in the pew. However, the notion of sacramental imagination is powerful and demands to be explored as such. Special attention is paid to the definition from *The Baltimore Catechism* and the need to identify Christ as the root metaphor. Emphasis is placed on three sacramental attitudes which appear to be most prevalent among Boomers and disconcerting for those in ministry. They are identified here as "Rules and Rubrics," "Magic," and "Me and Thee."

Chapter 3, *Sacramental Crisis for the Religious Educator (and Parents, Too)*, brings to light what I believe is at the heart of most parish controversies today. This also underscores the need for a paradigm shift in religious education/formation. My research shows that more than 95% of parents bringing their children for the reception of the sacraments today are Baby Boomers. While this generation certainly appears to be more educated, more outspoken and more demanding than any before, their limited sacramental imagination and experience undermine their religious desires for their children. Indeed, the most difficult dilemma facing religious educators is catechizing the future Church (our children) with today's Church (current theological practices and teachings). These children are often going home to either old Church (the Church parents think they remember) or no Church (adults in the home have long ago dropped out).

Chapter 4, *Assisting Faith Development: Implications for Present and Future Religious Formation*, is intended to give hope. It is through the reinterpretation of shared traditions, even argument and conflict concerning them, that we discover how our Church is still constituted by significantly shared meanings. This section takes a look at some theories and practices which assist in one's faith development. Recommended guidelines for reaching and evangelizing Baby Boomers and their families are outlined.

Chapter 5, *Summation and Conclusion: Reaction and Actions Taken*, is a summation of this study with some additional observations. To demonstrate the impact this study has had on my own work as a director of religious education, I've included brief overviews of two programs I developed and implemented utilizing this research. A reflective thought for the journey serves to summarize this labor and gives impetus for the continued quest to sacramental wholeness.

Chapter One

Defining the Baby Boomer Generation

Post World War II babies were conceived with a sense of optimism; born into a society determined to give them more than any preceding generation; they grew up during the Age of Aquarius, Transcendental Meditation, television evangelists, and a kaleidoscope of New Age spiritualities. They have often been stereotyped as self-centered, educated illiterates, morally decayed and spiritually bankrupt. They are the Baby Boomers – 76 million strong.[1] They are entering midlife and after a highly publicized absence are returning to Church. As those in ministry open doors and arms to welcome Boomers in the pews, they must also brace themselves for the challenges this group brings.

Defining the Baby Boomer generation is a task in itself. While this generation defies generalizations, there are some specific trends which can be identified. First I direct the reader's attention to the need to look at where Boomers came from. Then I will compare the two waves of Boomers and identify four economic/vocational trends and lifestyles. This section concludes with an examination of the Boomer spirituality in relation to the Catholic Church.

Boomers: Sociologically

Between 76 and 77 million babies were born in the United States between 1946 and 1964.[2] There are two possible clues to the boom. First, there was the end of World War II in 1945. It was a "popular" war and the troops came home victorious and secure in the notion that the United States was safe. Secondly, the dream of owning a house became a reality. The GI Loan Bill had been approved and homes could be purchased for less than $100 down and $100 per month. Secure in the fact that the United States was safe, people were eager to fill those new homes with the sounds of tiny feet. This era was known as Happy Days. Happy Days lasted for eighteen years and ended almost as abruptly as it began. No one knows for sure what stopped the Baby Boom, just as no one knows what sustained it for nearly two decades. However, it should be noted that the advent of birth control pill usage among American women in 1963 parallels the end of the boom.[3,4]

Since Baby Boomers comprise the biggest generation ever, there has been crowding at every stage of life, causing revolutions in fads and fashion, music and culture, politics and education. From conception through adolescence and young adulthood, Boomers' life experiences and lifestyles have been drastically different from their parents. This generation has transformed the work place, the role of women and the definition of family. In addition to their large population, the external factors of the times have had a significant impact on their lives and those around them.

Two Waves

In graphing the births of this generation, it is important to note there are actually two waves (see plates 1 and 2). The lives and attitudes of these two waves have been shaped significantly by their different life experiences.[5]

First Wave Boomers were born between 1946 and 1956. As school children in the 1950s, First Wave Boomers had bomb drills and watched the vastness of the world shrink with the advent of television. From their living rooms, they witnessed the assassination of President John F. Kennedy. Many participated in freedom marches and riots. These are the Boomers who were drafted and sent to fight in Vietnam. Students at home protested at campuses and military installations. Riots at universities and in political arenas seemed to demonstrate their frustration and lack of trust in institutions. In their late teens and early twenties, Boomers confronted the upheavals of the decade head on. Many were completely traumatized; all were in some way transformed by what happened. The counterculture of the 1960s provided drugs, rock and roll, and casual sex as an escape from the turmoil of everyday life. A great many became passionate visionaries, joining Campus Crusade for Christ or New Jerusalem and establishing various communes.

Those born between 1956 and 1964 comprise the Second Wave. Vietnam and campus riots were a part of their history books rather than their life experiences. They were still young when Martin Luther King, Jr., and Robert F. Kennedy were assassinated. Their late 1970s adolescence was marked by gas lines, the Three Mile Island nuclear accident and Watergate.

They came of age in a quieter time marked by environmental scares and economic recessions. The 1960s took on a mythic reality even for the Second Wave Boomers, and, although the impact was not as great, it remained significant. While their older siblings saw the rapid, chaotic change as revolution or revelation, the younger ones saw it more as something to which they must adapt, resigning themselves to the chaos around them rather than contesting it.

Education

Baby Boomers are the most highly educated of all generations. They were the first generation to have a choice in course selection in high school. Twice as many Boomers went to college compared to their parents, three times as many as their grandparents.[6] Their educational experiences provided them with life opportunities and experiences completely alien to previous generations. Their collegiate revolutions changed not just campus life but the focus of curriculum and criteria as well. Curriculum became more here and now rather than a classical, philosophical exploration. Colleges began realigning their mission statements to match the demands of the career bound students. These greater educational opportunities expanded choices in careers and lifestyles.

Here & Now

Currently Baby Boomers comprise one-third of the population. By the year 2000 their generation will make up half of the population.[7] Today few remnants of the impassioned 60s and early 70s exist, but the effects on Boomers remain. Diversity remains constant as their trademark. For many, challenge and change appear to be both motivation and goal. Due to the abrupt contrast between Boomers and their parents, some rather brash judgments have been made. Boomers have been labeled as the Generation of Choices, a Generation of Seekers, a Culture of Disbelievers, self-absorbed individuals, and Godless Creatures.[8] Perhaps their approaches to life justify these labels.

And, yet, in contrast to these labels, it has been noted that this generation is one of the most charitable. One has only to look at the many telethons, walks and the countless fund drives which generate billions of dollars each year. The Peace Corps and Habitat for Humanity are actual experiences in the lives of Boomers.

In contrast to their parents and grandparents, midlife career changes are the norm. When their parents were turning fifty, they were well on the way to retirement. Their children were mostly grown, out of the house and starting families of their own. For Boomers nearing fifty, their future looks quite different. Retirement is far off. No longer is the mandatory age sixty-five. Many work places have down sized forcing Boomers from upper and middle management positions to seek new employment or go back to school.

A new label has been introduced for Boomers: Sandwich Generation. It is no longer the rare household which contains parents, grandparents and children. Generation Xers are living at home longer than did their parents. People in general live longer today than they did fifty years ago. Consequently, Boomers are also charged with the care of their elderly or infirmed parents while still parenting their own children. The choice of caring for the parents at home or placing them in a nursing home is not a matter Boomers take lightly. Finances often force the issue. Such a living arrangement adds more stress to the already chaotic lifestyle of the Boomer.

3Ds looking for the 3Cs

Coming of age during a period of cultural chaos has caused the Boomers to move rather cautiously into adulthood. Baby Boomers have a 3D lifestyle and are looking for the 3Cs. The 3Ds of Baby Boomers are delayed marriage, deferred child bearing and soaring divorce rates. Now at midlife, and contrary to what their behavior indicates, they are seeking community, connections and commitment.[9] The older Boomers tend to be the "challengers," ready to take on the "establishment." The younger ones are the "calculators." They approach institutions with apathy. Intent on setting priorities for what to seek in a world where one cannot have it all,[10] they simply discard what they perceive as out of reach or as having little bearing on their life.

Boomers' overwhelming suspicion and lack of trust in institutions remain apparent.[11] Most still remain somewhat distanced from almost every institution, whether it is the military, banks, public schools, government or organized religion. A 1984 Gallup Poll found that Baby Boomers are the least trusting of all age groups toward social and political institutions, even less than people younger than themselves.[12] For many, the counterculture is still "where it's at." But a large percentage have abandoned or "dressed up" their counter cultural image.

Economics/Vocations

The inaccurate labeling of this generation persists. Just as in the late 60s and early 70s Boomers were often identified as Hippies, now many hold that the term Yuppy (Young Urban Professional) is synonymous with Baby Boomer. While the Boomer generation is more affluent than its ancestors (and, in all probability, than many future generations), it has more unequal distribution of income among its members.

Yuppies make up only 4 to 6% of the Boomer population. Yuppies are defined as self-assured, confident, on the leading edge, trend setters, dominant in the public forum and conspicuous consumers. They are professionals with managerial occupations and high incomes. Kirk McNeill's research further divides the Boomers into three more categories: Elite Workers, Workers, and Would-be's. The Elite Workers who comprise 14 to 16% of the Boomers and rate as second-highest income earners, are skilled technicians, mostly men. They are politically conservative and endorse traditional values. They lack the confidence of the Yuppies. They are also the "silent majority in the affluent market."

Eighty percent of the Boomers are considered to be on the low end of the income scale. In fact, the average Boomer income is $15,000. (They offset their income with "plastic.") The Workers make up the bulk of the mass market even among Boomers. McNeill says that they don't fit the stereotype at all. They are the least optimistic, least satisfied with their lives, most cynical and most conservative. Other authors have referred to this group as NewCollar, estimating that they compose one-third of the Boomer Generation.

The remaining group is the Would-be's. They have high educational levels, but low income. Their occupations consist of high school teachers, school counselors and others of similar nature. These Boomers choose these types of occupations because to them other values are more important than material goods.[13] While this group receives little media attention, they outnumber the Yuppies by eight times.

Values

It is the Baby Boomer values and lifestyles that are called into judgment more than anything else by non-Boomers. This generation appears to have replaced the nation's self-denial ethic with an ethic of self-fulfillment. To Boomers, life is intrinsically good in and of itself and should be lived fully and deeply. Not seeking self-fulfillment is viewed as a missed opportunity to live. Boomers believe that life is meant to be emotionally expressed and strive to "get in touch with one's feelings." These therapeutic attitudes and relationships, further detailed in Robert Bellah's works, *Habits of the Heart* and *The Good Society*, are observations on the current United States value system and its effects on society as a whole.

Bellah also demonstrates one of the inconsistencies/contradictions of the Baby Boomers which is relevant here. In his discussion on individualism he states that Boomers see a need for the very community of Church which their moral logic undercuts. Parents advocate "values" for their children even when they do not know what those "values" are.[14] Studies consistently demonstrate that this advocacy of values has been one of the major catalysts for Boomers to stay in/return to a traditional religion.

Boomers and Religion

According to statistics the Boomer spiritual life cycle is no different from previous generations;[15] however, Boomers see religion in somewhat different ways than their parents did. They have a greater concern for spirituality, for connectedness and for unity. They are in search of a vision which encompasses the body and spirit, the material as well as the immaterial. Boomers seek a connection as to how their lives as a whole not just their beliefs and practices take on meaning and direction. Most Boomers draw a distinction between "spirit" and "institution." In fact many consider themselves either religious or spiritual, seeing the spirit as an inner experiential aspect of religion, while institution is viewed as the outer, established form of religion.[16] Boomers are quick to separate the notions of belief and faith from faith and religion.

As Baby Boomers return to traditional religious their impact will be as significant here as in other venues they have entered. In fact, as we enter into the next millennium, their impact will be more significant. Wade Clark Roof's book, *A Generation of Seekers*, suggests that the Boomers have four major spiritualities: Loyalists, Returnees, Believers-but-not-belongers, and Seekers. Roof identifies a fifth group who refuses to acknowledge themselves as religious or spiritual.[17] For the purpose of this research Believers-but-not-belongers and Seekers are included under the heading of Dropouts. Loyalists are those who never left the Church (at least not physically). Returnees left for a while and then came back. Greeley's research demonstrates that this "vacation" from Church/organized religion parallels previous generations. However, once again, their sheer numbers made the Boomer absence more apparent. Boomer Returnees were often more involved in the anti-establishment movements of the sixties and thus more aligned with the values of that era.[18] Because these Returnees were affected more by the new generational values, they are less likely to be loyal to the institutional portion of organized religion. Returnees are proven to be less active in parish life. In the third category, the Dropouts, are those who dropped out completely, but may or may not come back to the Church for "rites of passage" such as baptism, marriage and funerals. These three types of spiritualities are present in today's Baby Boomer Catholics in varying degrees.

Loyalists

Andrew Greeley says the large percentage of Catholic Loyalists exists because Catholics "like" being Catholic. "Loyalty holds Catholics in their Church despite what the leaders say and do and because loyalty seems an eminently rational choice in a society that has historically been both devout and pluralistic. Indeed the tenacity and the rationality of such loyalty make the words and deeds of leaders usually quite irrelevant when religious choice is at issue."[19]

Catholic Loyalists may be conservative or liberal in their practices. For most, their theology is what some refer to as "cafeteria style," picking and choosing what dogmas they can actually live out. In interviews with Baby Boomers and their ministers, a large percentage of what can be termed *pew potatoes* were identified. These are the people who have remained loyal to the Church physically by fulfilling their Sunday obligation and/or making sure that their children are enrolled in some form of religious instruction. Beyond that, their commitment to their parish and their own faith journey is dormant.[20]

There is also a large active portion of Catholic Boomers who embraced the teachings of Vatican II. For them it was the Church coming alive with the Spirit breathing new life. As the world was changing, so, too, was their Church. With the changes Boomers could feel their desire for life and faith connectedness being met. These Loyalists seek parishes where laity involvement is welcomed and nourished. They are heavily involved in Renew groups, Small Christian Communities, Rite of Christian Initiation for Adults and various study groups. They are not afraid to join parishes where faith is put into action.

For others, Vatican II was symptomatic of an unstable Church caught up in an unstable world. In fact one Boomer tersely wrote, "My fondest hope is that one day I will awake to find that Vatican II was just a terrible nightmare." There is also a great deal of speculation among these Loyalists that the New Catechism will bring American Catholics back to their senses and Vatican rule. While many conservative Loyalists unhappily remain in liberal parishes, many more worship in churches which promote long-held traditions such as Latin Masses or seek parishes which do not challenge or conflict with their deep rooted religious beliefs.

As in every other institution, in the Church there are the middle of the road Loyalists. They make up a large percentage often labeled as the silent majority. They want to grow in their faith, but now is not the right time. They are caught in a balancing act of obligations: work, family, etc. Well aware that faith is a gift, they remain open but not actively seeking. Their faith growth happens rather then being actively pursued. For this group, motivation by obligation is not distasteful, but merely a fact of life.

Returnees

Returnees make up 25% of the total Catholic population.[21] Like their Protestant neighbors, there are two specific motives for their return: midlife introspection and a desire to give their children morals and values. But there is also a third and what may be held as the most powerful reason, the graced nature of the Church's sacraments (Chapters II and III will elaborate). Even for those who are unable to comfortably articulate their own sacramental experience, they are deeply committed to having their children participate in these ritualized rites of passage. For this is the religious heritage they wish to pass on to their children. This, they contend, is their religious right of being a Catholic.

Returnees to the Catholic Church can be easily traumatized if not received pastorally. They are usually easy to identify by the questions they ask: "What happened to the black box [confessional]?" "What do you mean the school isn't run by nuns?" "Why doesn't the Bishop slap the candidate for confirmation?" Their reaction to the response of these questions may be extreme: a calming of the spirit or a complete uprooting of their beliefs. Greeley says that many Boomers left to explore or because the Church leadership failed to live up to their spiritual vision. After a break, these Returnees decide that their religion is a birthright and that no hierarchy can stand between them and their faith. Their reception of the changes and current trends is diverse. "Wonderful!" "Great." "Had I known that confession emphasizes reconciliation rather than my guilt, I would not have stayed away so long." "Where do I go to sign the petition to get rid of this Director of Religious Education and her ideas about not having separate First Communion Masses for our school children? Doesn't she know that this time it's a sacrament?" "They have ruined my Church."

Parishes often have a desire to "fix" these Returnees by "correcting" their theology. Well intended preservers of the faith establish obvious barriers under the guise of guidelines, which are imposed with grim legalism upon those who wish to have their children receive the sacraments. Instead of their return or their reentry being a celebration, it becomes a succession of hoops one must jump through or an administrative test to be passed. These are perceived as roadblocks or punishments to the Returnees. For many it affirms the reasons why they left originally.

Returnees make up the largest percentage of Baby Boomers in the pews today. There are those who return with a hope of finding that sense of identity and community they experienced as a child, that sense of awe they had when they first received communion. Faith seemed more visible and tangible to them then. Church was simpler than the chaotic world in which they now reside. They are shocked to find out that the Church of their youth no longer exists. Meeting the Returnee and pastorally walking with him or her may be the greatest challenge faced in ministry.

The thrust of the Second Vatican Council teachings is that the sacraments are acts of faith which require and presuppose faith. However, these Returnees for the sacraments seem to exhibit little or no faith understanding. And yet, these same Council documents also teach that participation in the sacraments has a nourishing and deepening impact on faith. Thus, parish leaders are faced with a dilemma: to challenge peripheral Catholics who present themselves (or their child) for a sacrament but not crush them with legalistic jargon and rules which serve only to further alienate them.[22]

Dropouts

This challenge is intensified only by the Dropouts. In 1960, 15% of those raised Catholic no longer identified themselves as such.[23] That figure has not changed much in the last quarter of a century. One-half of the defectors joined other religions, usually in conjunction with marriage. Once again, there are varying degrees of Dropouts in the Catholic Church. There are the "C and E" Catholics, those who attend Mass only on Christmas and Easter, usually refraining from receiving the Eucharist. There are the "Drop 'em Off and Run" Catholics. These are the parents who hold that religion is good for you when you're young. They got their dosage growing up and they are making sure they drop their children off at religion classes so they can get their dose. While this situation is often apparent in the CCD population, there is indication that it is a significant factor for parochial school enrollment as well. Mass attendance is seen as nonessential for many families whose children attend religious education classes. "I just can't drag my kids to both CCD and Mass." "My child attends Mass during school. That is his worshiping community. What's all fuss about attending Sunday Mass?"

Then there are the Drop-in/Dropouts. They dropped out in their late teens or mid-twenties, dropping back in for the sacraments of matrimony and infant baptism of their children. The motivation is often purely secular. "I've always dreamed of a big Church wedding. What's the name of that Church on the corner with the pretty stained glass windows?" Grandparents still hold a great deal of clout as well: "You have to get the baby baptized. After all you don't want to disappoint the family." Catholic Dropouts also tend to return as their children reach the age[24] for the sacraments of First Communion and Confirmation.[25] Their children can often be tracked by their religion class attendance: weekly in grade two; sporadic in the third and fourth grades; nonexistent in grades five, six, and seven; and waiting in line for enrollment into grade eight. The question often arises among religious educators and clergy, "Do you let the children in, praying for the best but knowing it's a socially graced moment the parents desire or just say, "No," thereby punishing the child and perhaps closing the door on a member of the future Church?" Roof would label their behavior as that of a Believerbut-not-a-Belonger more than as a Seeker, but for many, this period renews or begins a time of seeking.

Again, Vatican II has a role to play in the dropout scene among Catholics. As one middle-aged Boomer stated, "Why bother to go to Church? They did away with limbo, guilt and the fear of God. What's the purpose? Anyway, I'm still covered. I went to ten First Friday Masses in a row." *For most First Wave Boomers, formation ended with Confirmation. They were already on the outside looking in when the wisdom of Vatican II began to be disseminated.* All they saw was the "doing away with" rather than a return to a fuller, people-centered Church.

In addition, there are the true Dropouts who never return to any formalized religion. They raise their children with values but do not identify them with any formalized religion. For Catholic Dropouts, defection has often been caused by unpleasant memories associated with priests and religious, disagreement with the Church's position on divorce and marriage, and the banning of some theologians by Rome. The intense media coverage of reported pedophilia among clerics will no doubt offer another reason for disillusionment. Among Boomers the birth control issue is not an underlying cause for dropping out. They feel that the role of the Pope is within the confines of the Church not within the bedroom.

For older Boomers and the prior generation it seems that whatever windows Vatican II had opened, *Humanae Vitae* slammed shut. The contrast on this issue between Boomers and their parents is clearly evidenced in one Boomer's response when asked to compare her parents in their stance/relationship to the hierarchical Church with her own. "My father was a devout Catholic with a great sense of integrity and fidelity to his Church. However, after eight children within a period of ten years, he realized my mother could just not cope with another pregnancy or child. He went against his Church for the welfare of his wife and utilized artificial birth control. While he continued to go to Mass, pray and follow all other religious customs of the time, from that moment on, he stopped participating in the celebration of the sacrament of Eucharist. Only on his death bed did he allow himself to receive communion." She relates this story out of a great love and respect for her father. Her father's relationship with the sacraments bound by a sense of guilt and legalism, instilled in him as a child, continued throughout his life, to the point where he denied himself participation in the eucharist. For herself, the practice of birth control does not preclude her participation in the sacraments. She believes her decision is not regulated by a Church leadership that does not understand but by a God that does.

Summary: Boomer as Spiritual Seekers

Roof's term "Seeker" came through in all of the groups interviewed. Many Boomer men and women Loyalists told of exploring other religions, especially those of the Eastern culture to give more depth to their spirituality and prayer life. The liberal loyalists seemed more open to finding what worked for them and then adjusting/accepting the various Church teachings that allowed them to continue within its framework. They are more concerned with the spirit of the law rather than the law itself. When confronted with a tough issue they are prone to ask, "What would Jesus do?" rather than "What does the Pope say about this?"

Liberal loyalists perceive that the Church now recognizes them as adults who have the ability to explore the teachings of the church and make conscientious decisions accordingly.

On the other hand, conservative loyalists cling tightly to church teachings. Tradition is the deciding factor. They crave the stability of a Church which has not changed in the past two thousand years. Modern practices, such as communion in the hand or communal penance services are purely symptomatic of the church in adolescence, a time for perseverance until reformation of the ancients. (Council of Trent or Pope Gregory)

Returnees, unlike the loyalists, made a conscious decision to put their church relationship on hold for a while. They often experience a form of culture shock upon their re-entrance into the Church of today. Many seeking a greater connection with scripture, speak of experimenting with other types of religions such as fundamentalism and Bible-centered practices. They continue sharing in ecumenical Bible study groups even after their return to Catholicism. They are delighted to see a greater emphasis on scripture within the liturgy but because of their absence have a hard time making the transition. There is an obvious gap in their religious understanding and yet there is an undeniable depth to their faith. Working with Returnees such as these can be at once exhilarating and exhausting.

Various Dropouts are also seeking, but their path is less direct and more unsure than that traveled by the Loyalists and Returnees. Their faith life is often clouded by their ties to secularism. Goal-oriented, the Dropout connection with church is based on the number of sacraments they have accumulated. "How many service hours to get confirmed?" "When is our responsibility to the poor fulfilled?" The challenge here is often helping them to uncover the presence of Christ and the church within their everyday lives so that they may see the connection between secular and religious – between worldly and Christ.

All Baby Boomers, spurred on by their complex and diverse formative years, educational opportunities and life styles, approach religion in the same manner: challenging, exploring, demanding, seeking. Their relationship with the Catholic Church is a sacramental one. Even the Believers-but-not-Belongers expressed a desire to share in these rituals of life passages. But like everything else, their understanding, approach and reception of the sacraments are as diverse as their culture. The uniform sacramental rituals of the 1950s and early 1960s stand in stark contrast to the diverse celebrations of today (and for many years to come). It is reflective of the variety of faith understandings found within the pews. The Boomer Church is summed up by James Joyce when he states, "Catholicism [today] means, 'here comes everyone.'"[26]

Are You a Boomer? Are the Majority of Your Congregation Baby Boomers?

What kind of Boomer are you? Are you a Loyalist, Returnee or a Dropout? Are the majority of the Boomers in your pews Loyalists, Returnees, Dropouts or a combination of all three? Answering the following questions may help you get a handle on your own faith identity and give you some direction to take with your parishioners.

1. Born:
   ___ Before 1946: Eisenhower Kid
   ___ Between 1946-55: First Wave Boomer
   ___ Between 1956-64: Second Wave Boomer
   ___ After 1964: Generation X

2. Education:
   ___ high school ___ technical school
   ___ some college ___ undergraduate degree
   ___ graduate degree

3. Marital Status: ___ single ___ divorced
   ___ married

4. Child/ren Age(s): ___ ___ ___ ___ ___

5. Religion:
   Roman Catholic (___ cradle, ___ convert)
   ___ Protestant ___ Jewish
   Other _____

6. My church attendance during my lifetime
   ____ has been consistent
   ____ included a period of absence
   ____ been somewhat sporadic (Holy days and
   Sacraments)

7. With regard to Vatican Rule and the role of the
   Pope, I
   ____ am loyal in all matters of doctrine.
   ____ adhere to most matters of doctrine.
   ____ think the Pope's role does not have
   significant impact on my faith.

8. My attitude toward church/parish involvement is that
   ____ I am obligated by faith commitment.
   ____ I am invited but I do not desire it at this time.
   ____ it is not for me.

9. I believe that Sacraments
   ____ are the focal point of Church existence.
   ____ renew my relationship with Christ.
   ____ are important to get.

10. I call myself Catholic because I am
    ____ Baptized and practice my faith.
    ____ Baptized and choose to continue.
    ____ Baptized.

11. For me, faith formation
    ____ means parents and children together.
    ____ is completed at confirmation.
    ____ means it is important for children to get the sacraments.
    ____ is a life long process.

12. Ways I find to deepen my faith:
    ____ personal reflection
    ____ no need at this time
    ____ studies with peers

Although the answers to these questions may vary and the tabulation won't clearly distinguish between Loyalists, Returnees and Dropouts, they will help the minister gain some insight as to the general complexion of the group and hopefully help identify a starting point and path.

The next section will look at the sacramental understandings of Boomers in light of their diversity and religious formation.

Chapter Two

Range of Sacramental Understanding among Catholic Baby Boomers

The Catholic Church is a sacramental community. It is a community which gathers to celebrate the presence of Christ in its midst. Gather five Catholic Baby Boomers to discuss sacraments and no fewer than five different operational theologies will emerge. Each of these will have varying degrees of understanding and obvious overlapping.

The following is intended to help the reader gain insights into the Catholic Baby Boomer's understanding of sacraments. We begin with a limited historical perspective. Then the components of sacramental imagination, ritual, community and narrative are explored. Next the external impact of the twentieth century and the internal reaction by theoreticians and practioners of the Church are identified as the primary catalysts of the current fragmentation of sacramental wholeness. The groundwork of this section leads to the identification and description of three sacramental attitudes most prevalent among Catholic Baby Boomers today.

History of the Sacraments

Catholics hold to the "sacramental principle." This principle affirms that God is manifested in a unique way through concrete symbols and rituals.[1] Through these we meet God in the natural world and within ourselves. Baby Boomers are not the first generation of the Church seeking a clearer understanding of the connectedness. They are not the first generation to lack wholeness in their sacramental understanding. In fact, the very nature of the term sacrament has been the source of theological controversy since the beginnings of the Church.

During the early centuries there was no intention to limit the number of sacraments to seven. Any ritual that celebrated a divine saving action was considered a mystery and a sacrament. Some lists of sacraments reached thirty in number. By the mid-thirteenth century the number was finally set at seven.[2] The Reformation of the 1500s challenged much of the Catholic sacramentality. Brennan Hill, a theology professor and well-known author, notes that the Catholics ran away with the sacraments while the Protestants ran away with the Bible. Thus, the Catholic tradition has long been rooted in its sacramental structure.

Thomas Aquinas, following the tradition of Augustine, understood the sacraments to be sacred signs: A sacrament is a sign of a sacred thing, insofar as it makes men holy.[3] Most older Roman Catholics grew up with *The Baltimore Catechism*'s definition: "A sacrament is an outward sign instituted by Christ to give grace."[4] While it speaks of Christ, this definition minimizes His role, focusing more on grace. Sacraments are presented as realities distinct from His person, rather than extensions of His life, death and resurrection.

Vatican II drew the understanding back to a wider definition of sacrament which includes the seven liturgical sacraments. These liturgical sacraments happen because humans are a sacrament. The work of the sacrament is effective because it has worked. It is affective because it is working. Sacraments engage all aspects of our being: head, heart, will, spirit and body. Today, few Catholics have encountered a wholistic sacramental engagement of their entire being or have recognized it as such.

Sacraments as Symbols

In his book, *From Magic to Metaphor*, George Worgul defines sacraments as "symbols arising from the ministry of Christ and continued in and through the Church, which when received in faith, are encounters with God; Father, Son and Spirit." He further states that sacraments are not merely signs, but symbolic signs.[5] They are the symbols of Christ's risen presence. The Church is the reality Christ instituted above and beyond any institution of sacraments. The sacraments are meaningful insofar as they are extensions of the Church. If a sacramental theology does not have a root metaphor of Christ's death and resurrection then it is inadequate and becomes irrelevant in one's spiritual faith life. Sacraments continually express and reinforce this Christian world view and, in doing so, bring all of reality under the paradigmatic Christ.[6]

Ritual Gateway to Imagination

According to George Worgul, the sacramental rituals touch a person's preconscious, giving way to one's mythic sense. They are the creation of the sacramental imagination. As one knows, imagination is stronger than knowledge, for it becomes a part of one's myth. Because pre-adolescents have not yet learned the language to communicate their sacramental experience, they make emotional connections to tangible "things" such as the scapular Aunt Ruth gave them. When their ritual ontology fails to develop, faith does not mature. Sacramental imagination is limited to their initial attitudes, severing opportunity for sacramental wholeness. (See Plate 4, Appendix.)

Andrew Greeley speaks of sacramental imagination as well. He states:

> Religion is an imaginative 'cultural system' – a Catholic's collection of directing 'pictures' through which humans organize and give meaning to the phenomena that impinges on their consciousness, especially insofar as these phenomena require some explanation of the ultimate meaning of life.[7]

Before religion became theology and philosophy, it was symbol and story, the poetry of religion. These speak to our aesthetic sense. It is through that poetry that the imagination of the whole human person is in many ways superior to the theological understanding of the sacraments. In fact, Greeley professes that it is one's Catholic sacramental imagination that keeps one Catholic.[8] It is this form of sacramental encounter which engages the faith and brings it into identity with the Church.

An article by Alex Garcia-Rivera also speaks to our mythic sense as he describes sacraments as "an entry into God's imagination."[9] Garcia-Rivera states that sacraments are not things to be explained but acts that engage us in a very special kind of imagination that flows from the origins of things.[10] This primal imagination "imagines" us into being. He explains that this sacramental imagination has the capability of changing our lives, allowing one to be re-created, re-imaged anew. The sacramental imagination invites the participant to see the world as it really is, to shift one from life present to God's presence. It allows one to give way to the life-death-resurrection experience again and again, while coming ever more into the reality of a life in Christ. The sacramental imagination changes the terms under which we exist, bringing innocence to a dangerous world, fellowship to places of abandonment, healing to the sick, and the way back to those who get lost in the complex and confusing world of the human condition.[11]

For Catholics, participation in the celebration of the sacraments keeps them rooted with the risen Christ. The Catholic sacraments are deepened by the components of symbol, ritual, community and heritage. A symbol points to a reality different from itself and makes it present without being identical to it. Symbols are primarily agents of unity and convergence. They "open up a level of reality, of being and corresponding meaning, which otherwise we could not reach, and in doing so that symbol participates in that which it opens to new awareness."[12] Symbols allow visible connectedness. They encourage one to reach out to the reality they hold, calling us to another place, another time, another being.

The sharing of these symbols through the familiar pattern of sacramental rituals holds the assembly together. Ritual is an indigenous to human cultural and psychological life. Psychological, sociological and anthropological research attests to the absolute necessity of ritual for personality development and mature integration. Ritual permeates three dimensions of culture: language, patterns of behavior, and social structures. It is an attempt to express meaning. Ritual is an a priori necessity for the very existence and sustenance of human culture and the Church's sacramental structure. Ritualistic language and gesture disclose meaning for the "odd" situations of life and give voice to the unspokenness of the sacrament. Ritualized patterns in sacraments evoke intimacy, interiorization, solidarity, and presence with the Christ.[13] Only when these "ties" are understood by the participants are they enabled to make connections to their fundamental values. The intended central role of sacramental ritual reveals the mystery of Christ working with the human, vascillating between continuity and change. As young Catholic children participate in the sacraments of initiation, these rituals become part and parcel of their identity. Their maturity and active continual participation in the rituals bring about their acquisition of sacramental wholeness, a life in Christ. While the ritual identity remains constant, our relationship and identity evolve, reflective of our own maturation in faith and under standing.

Community

Humans have an innate need to belong and form community. They seek out those who share commonalities, especially their faith beliefs. Common beliefs bring people together to celebrate as a community. The community, constituted by symbols and rituals, continues by transmitting these to its members. It is a group of people who interact through their shared story. Community is also seen as the protector of the religious heritage. Sacramentally the Christian community is seen as the Body of Christ. Just as Christ nurtures and gives sustenance, so too, does the community. The community, the assembly of the faithful, is the visible expression of the Church.

Without community, the story cannot continue. Without community, one cannot grow or further develop. Without community, one ceases to exist.

Narrative

Before formalized religious formation and ritualistic participation, faith heritage was (and still is) powerfully passed on by story and narrative shared within the community. It is the sharing of this faith, guided by the Holy Spirit that has kept it alive for more than two thousand years. Imagination is enhanced by shared stories and narratives. How one images him/herself with others, community and Christ is determined by the imagination. Story and narrative give one the imaginative power to be transformed to another place and time. Narratives touch where logical intellect cannot travel. Sacraments are the narratives of the Christian mystery.

Narratives are always works in progress with each storyteller injecting his or her own cultural understanding. As each adds his or her own inflection or style, the original meaning is altered or, in extreme cases, lost entirely. As the human narrative has evolved, the Church has responded by emphasizing various sacramental theologies. Worgul identifies two factors that have contributed to didactic shifts in sacramental formation, celebration and understanding. The human narrative, culture, is an external factor while the theoreticians and practitioners within the Church makes up the internal factor. These have contributed to didactic shifts in sacramental formation, celebration and understanding. It is these internal and external factors which cry out for balance. Seeking balance of faith calls one back to the greatest narrative of all, Scripture.

Fragmenting the Understanding of Sacraments

External Factors

The twentieth century entered a cultural age with new and different presuppositions about the meaning, purpose and style of life. Structures of the cultural-philosophical system, upon which the former theology of the sacraments was based, eroded. In a society that questions everything institutional, it is difficult for the Church to sustain questions and objections raised against previous sacramental syntheses. Due to the varying theological and cultural shifts, the discipline is often perceived as existing in confusion, if not chaos.

The twentieth century has been labeled as an "age of crisis": economic, transportation, environmental, fuel, identity, marriage, sex and gender roles. No other generation has lived so fully in an age of crisis as the Baby Boomer. Worgul and leading sociologists see the explanation as threefold. First, society is suffering from mass neurosis: sociosis.[14] A quest for individualism is impeding formation of a necessary stability and integration of social life. This is especially true in the Baby Boomer Generation where for many the interaction of the extended families and small close knit communities has evaporated. Second, humankind is circumscribed by crisis and condemned to alienation. Boomers, raised within a country which promotes moral individualism have found themselves isolated and thirsting for community.[15] Third, the twentieth century is a rare time of human history. People are living simultaneously through the dying process of a past culture and the gestation period of a new self-understanding of humankind. The whole core and foundations of the culture are being recast.[16]

Culture is a multiple layering of diversified elements including language, institutions, social behaviors and religious beliefs. The perception of reality by social groups expressed in and through its social institutions and their patterns of behavior are diverse and often diametrically opposed. Culture is essentially dependent on the element of certain unconscious principles and beliefs which ground and sustain what is expressed in a conscious fashion in social institutions and patterns of behavior. When these cultural elements collide, their social institutions collapse or become countercultural to the world around them.

American Catholics were raised in an immigrant Church with many traditions based on ethnicity

rather than solid Catholic teachings. As neighbor-
hoods changed with the integration of various races
and nationalities, parishes reshaped their identities
to include these new members. As families move to
the suburbs, the small ethnic parishes, which often
served as extended families, have virtually disap-
peared. Yet, the existence of some "pocket" communities stands in contrast to the large parish melting
pots and offer solace to those seeking a clearer sense
of belonging. The decline of ethnic parishes caused
the loss of some important, long standing religious
traditions.

Internal Factors

Internally, theoreticians and practitioners of the
Church reorganized and accommodated themselves
to the cultural shift. They attempted to rebuild a
sacramental theology based on the new cultural presuppositions. This theology contained a certain abandonment and dismantling of the former synthesis,
requiring a temporal process, a tentative grasping,
which resisted any *fait accompli* or total replace-
ment.[17]

This generated reactions resulting in various
"theological" attitudes emerging which either mini-
mize or dismiss the wholeness of the sacramental
engagement. The focus on developing an academic
understanding of sacrament perpetuated a vertical
sacramental involvement rather than a horizontal
relationship. In cooperation and/or retaliation,
catechetical studies focused on a segment of theology
rather than a wholistic formation, causing further
splintering. Three fragmented attitudes seem to appear most prevalent today.[18] Unfortunately these at-

titudes touted as sacramental theology have effectively reduced the sacramental imagination and thus one's rootedness to Christ.

Three Forms of Boomer Sacramentality

Rules and Rubrics

First, there is the older, mechanical model of sacramental interpretation and formation. Here the meaning of the Christian ritual is reduced by equating it to rubrics. In this case, attention is lured away from the real significance of Christian sacraments as an expression of the root metaphor of Christ and focused on the style, directions, or "smoothness" of the ceremony. "The faithful believe that if they do it [the sacramental celebration] right, they will be closer to God." This is most reflective of first wave Boomers catechized with *The Baltimore Catechism.* When asked what they remember about their First Communion, "straight lines, no chewing the bread, proper attention to genuflecting, hands folded in an upward motion" make up the top items listed. Confirmation preparation consisted of memorizing certain sections of the catechism. Determination of readiness consisted of passing "the test." Desire and openness are irrelevant. It is the duty of the Soldier of Christ to protect the Church from heretics, just as it is the duty of the good Catholic parent to make sure that their babies were baptized. It is a good Catholic's responsibility to do his or her Easter duty. As Barry Mersmann, an archdiocesan associate director of religious education stated, "Catholics back then knew how to do the sacraments but didn't know why and for that matter weren't allowed to ask."

Following the rules means baptizing the baby as soon as possible even to the exclusion of the recovering mother. Confession of sin (whether venial or mortal) must preclude entrance into the celebration of the Eucharist. Confirmation can only occur if the candidate has fulfilled the required amount of service hours and memorized the Apostles' Creed. The sacrament of marriage may be bestowed if both members of the couple are practicing Catholics. For many rule and rubric followers their attendance to Sunday Mass suffices for their religious life.

Magic

The second prevalent attitude is marked by the ingredient of magic and focused on the concept of grace. Grace is understood as God's life in relation with the world. It is the meeting of Christ, the reclaiming of his presence.[19] Number 1997 from the *New Catechism of the Catholic Church,* 1994, states that "Grace is a *participation in the life of God."* It is this participation in a life with God that changes our being. Number 1996 states, "Our justification comes from the grace of God. Grace is *favor,* the *free and undeserved help* that God gives us to respond to his call . . . " This emphasizes the concrete helps of grace.

The Catechism continues to outline grace as a "gratuitous gift, *sanctifying* and *deifying."* Unfortunately this hard to understand concept took on "mystical qualities" and gave birth to the concept of magical sacraments. Grace became more related to the soul rather than the body. The focus was on the "stuff" of grace as opposed to the life altering participation.

Boomers who profess this orthodoxy tend to have been catechized just prior to and immediately following Vatican II. These Boomers tend to be from the middle of the two waves: late first wavers and early second wavers. Teaching the *Baltimore Catechism* was passé, but the wisdom of Vatican II had not yet been developed in instructional materials for faith formation of little ones preparing for the initiation sacraments. Practitioners knew that our ritualistic actions were graced by Christ. So they began focusing on this grace.

In this attitude, the relational understanding of grace gives way to a concentration on grace as power. Sacraments are viewed as "magical, mystical tours"[20] taking one away from the realities of post industrial life, an escape. For some, Christ's presence became limited to the sacramental elements alone, sharing stories of eucharistic banquets where bread and wine were transformed into actual flesh. In the abdication of this stance, sacraments are reduced to "dated," "primitive," and "archaic" behaviors belonging to a previous era, but the notion of grace remains magically skewed. Still seen as a power of God, the notion of grace shifts to a quantitative measure of Christ. There becomes then a desire to move from rules and regulations to collecting graces. One can receive graces from many prescribed things in the Church, but grace attained through the sacraments means the most. As one Boomer reflected, "The more graces one could collect, the better seat he or she would get in heaven."

Religious educators have a tendency to identify sacramental understanding of this nature as "Zap" theology. Parents catechized in this theology today see little or no need for much faith formation, just give the child the sacrament. Thousands of babies were baptized not for the sake of preserving the faith but to protect them from the state of limbo. Confirmation was viewed as a fortification of the child against evil. One distraught mother appeared at a Religious Education Commission meeting urging the members to return the celebration of the sacrament to the eighth grade. After all, "there are many high school girls getting pregnant these days." Many, who subscribe to this theological understanding, hold that if the priest is holy enough, if the religious education administrator is religious enough and if the bishop is truly consecrated, their child's confirmation will indeed cure the sin of adolescence. Some think of their Catholic wedding as that magic moment when the sacrament occurred rather than seeing their marriage as a continuous sacrament of grace and commitment.

Me and Thee

The third sacramental attitude found among Boomers which can be identified dichotomizes the community and the individual. In this situation, the Christian ritual identified is so strongly connected with the individual that the community becomes expendable and is often excluded. Usually the tendency is to reduce the sacraments to private affairs, excluding the communal aspect. Taken to its ultimate conclusion, the necessity of ritual vanishes as an extrinsic and a "Me and Thee" mentality takes over. Second wave Boomers seem to exhibit this attitude more than older Boomers, further propelled by their American individualism. Catechesis had moved from ritual regulations and the tallying of graces to emphasizing a personal relationship with God. The primary catechesis for pre-adolescents was what some refer to as "fluff" while one religious education consultant has nicknamed it the "Chaotic Collage" period. All the teachers had to do was tell the children to love God, love your family and yourself, love your neighbor, make a collage about love and class was over and you could then "get" the sacrament.

The Jesus and me practices ran high in the late seventies and eighties as separate First Communion Masses for the school children and the CCD children were held. The idea was that smaller groups of children would allow for the individual child to more fully come into being "with" Jesus. The popular holy card of Jesus giving the host to the First Communicant seems to typify this theological stance. Baptisms became private affairs done in the afternoon with the absence of the Church community. Some think Confirmation is strictly an individual affair, not related to their future life in community. This was well expressed by parents who complained that raising the age would require their children to have to return to the parish once they had already completed grade school. No wonder the understanding of Confirmation is in such a state of flux or so aptly put, "a sacrament in search of a theology." Sadly, in this Me and Thee understanding, a wholistic sacramental theology and the role of community are both lost.

In all three of these theologies, Rules and Rubrics, Magic, and Me and Thee, the priest is seen as the intermediator between the sinful lay person and Christ. The sacramental essence happens "to" rather than "with." There appears to be no link between the participants, Jesus' ministry and Christology. The sacramental ritual is methodical and the person's response is mechanical in nature. There is a philosophical deficiency of the "Presence of the Risen Christ" within the community. These attitudes undermine the sacraments as rites, rituals, community in action and celebrations. Sacraments experienced with these attitudes become stumbling blocks on the pathway of sacramental imagination, completely destroying the balance between personal relationship and communal presence. If one's sacramental attitude remains at the level of one of these skewed understandings, if it presupposes belief and faith in the reality-event, then there is a danger of the sacraments becoming empty rituals devoid of Christ's presence. Here again, these persistent attitudes among Boomers seem to belie their relationship divided with religion and faith.

Empowering the faithful to move beyond these fragmented sacramental understandings is the quest of the Church. Evangelizing those currently in the pews demands an attention to developing and experiencing a fuller understanding of the Sacraments and a sacramental life. Indeed, obtaining sacramental wholeness will renew, energize and pave the path of Church for the next millennium.

The next chapter demonstrates what happens when these fragmented sacramental attitudes left unattended are brought to their ultimate conclusion.

Chapter Three

■ ■ ■ ■ ■ ■

Sacramental Crisis for the
Religious Educator
(And Parents, Too)

As seen in Chapter 1, since Boomers grew up when the entire world, the Church not withstanding, was in a state of flux, their relationships are diverse and very much separate from previous generations. Their spiritual journey is reflective of their secular lifestyle. For most Baby Boomers – Loyalists, Returnees and Dropouts alike – their understanding of the sacraments remains limited, intact with their "kiddie sacramental" experience. The previous section identified three sacramental attitudes which prevail among Boomers and have skewed their sacramentality. These fragmented sacramental understandings have created the greatest distress for those ministering to Boomers and for the Boomers themselves. *Herein lies the crisis: for while the Church views sacraments through a theological perspective of rites and rituals, many Baby Boomers have reduced sacramental celebrations to rights and parties.* It is this clashing of ideologies which will be discussed in this section.

Sacramental Rights

The Unfinished Business of Kiddie Sacraments

Brennan Hill refers to the sacraments of Initiation (Baptism, Eucharist and Confirmation) as the "kiddie sacraments."[1] I find this term to be most appropriate since these sacraments are received during childhood, and for many Boomers, their sacramental understanding remains as it was learned during these initiation sacrament experiences. As Loyalists, Returnees and Dropouts bring their children to participate in the sacraments, one can be assured that there will be a collision between parental expectations and current Church practices. When one's sacramental understanding, formed in childhood, is called into question, the person becomes threatened and sees his or her faith as challenged. This can lead to abandonment, alienation or, hopefully, growth. The response is determined by how pastorally the Boomer is confronted and how receptive he or she is.

For Boomers, the Church's formational focus has been visibly concentrated on children. The message of adult formation is new and seems in complete contrast to what was espoused a few short years ago. Although Boomers view life as a journey of continuous improvement and growth, their religious life does not parallel. Sacramental ritual is a constant challenge to work on completing the "unfinished business" begun at the sacramental moment. A personal adherence to Jesus and a continual conversion of one's whole life to the message of the Gospel is the Catholic Christian message. Christian faith is an active adherence and total commitment to the person of Jesus as the ultimate revelation of God and therefore, the ultimate meaning of life.[2] This message was not emphasized in the sacramental formation of most Boomers.

The Church tends to operate under the assumption that the faithful's faith journey has always been a continual one. In each age period, additional sacramental values are to be introduced through ritual behavior and formation enhanced by the person's personal and psychological development. One's understanding would be guided and reinforced in succeeding stages of adult ritual behavior.[3] Thus it is thought that the repetitive, interpersonal and adaptive ritualistic behavior would further develop into sacramental wholeness.

This assumption fails to take into account the religious life cycles of Americans and the impact of their life experiences, especially their lack of sacramental ritual repetition. Ultimately, most adult sacramental understanding remains as it was with their initial experience (see plate 3). A limited ritual experience cannot lead to a mature understanding or further the sacramental imagination. This underdeveloped sacramental imagination limits one's relationship with Christ's presence both in the sacraments and within the community. Consequently, the clash between current sacramental teachings and celebrations and parental desires/demands have brought the sacramental crisis to light. The crisis is not limited only to those being ministered to but also found among those doing the ministering.

Secular Sacraments

For many Boomers in the pews today, their experience with the sacraments is limited by one or more of the

attitudes outlined in Chapter 2. For them, the sacraments are something to which people have a right
and display reverence. Sacraments are individualistic
and social opportunities devoid of the root metaphor
of Christ – empty rituals. With *believing* disjointed
from *living*, it becomes a portable faith. This has led
to a fourth attitude, to which Worgul only alludes:
sacramental participation as a secular event rather
than a theological ritual. The rites are participated
in purely as social celebrations for "rites of passage."
The focus is on dress, parties, who's invited and
presents as opposed to Christ's presence. In main-
taining this secular attitude, the individualist's reaction to communal celebrations is one of disdain. After
all, "How can the Church accommodate my guests
with all those other people there?" Baptism is seen
as an opportunity to celebrate the baby's birth and
get presents. The celebration of First Communion is
identified by one Director of Religious Education as
the "Catholic Cotillion." Appearance and social ap-
propriateness reign: "I spent a lot of money on my
daughter's dress and she should be in the front for
the picture." Confirmation has become the "sacrament of exodus" in that it is a graduation from religion
classes. "Let's move Confirmation to high school so
we can keep the kids in school/CCD longer."

The following answering machine message was
proposed by a frustrated pastor and myself in reaction
to continued confrontations by a group of Baby
Boomers seeking to have the sacraments "their way."
It was developed through enlightenment from parent
sacramental meetings and tales from other religious
educators.

> Church of the Pick and Choose Sacraments. Bap-
> tism, will be conducted this Saturday in conjunc-

tion with our Boosters' Car Wash. Remember to leave your child's window down. For those who find our liturgies too lengthy, we've installed a Communion Automatic Teller Machine. Push 1 if you wish to receive just the host, 2 for the wine or 3 for a combination. Confirmation can now be done by mail. Just send in your name, address and saint's name. Tell us in two sentences or less why you would like to be confirmed and we'll mail back your certificate. Make sure to include a self-addressed, stamped envelope. Due to a lack of penitents, we've shortened the hours for our drive thru confessional. Toot and Tell will now be open on Saturdays from 4:00 to 4:05 p.m. Have a good day.

This "nouveau" Catholic Church answering machine message speaks in response to the sacramental crisis being felt in parishes today. It demonstrates a parish caught between an attempt to adhere to the mandate of Vatican Council II which seeks to renew the sacraments as the living center of Catholic spiritual life and a community whose sacramentality is weak, fragile and in disarray.

As religious educators seek to respond to the mandates of Vatican II, they face a most difficult dilemma: preparing the future Church (the children) with today's Church (current theological practices and teachings) in a setting in which children are often going home to either old Church (the Church parents think they remember) or no Church (adults in the home have long ago dropped out). Religious educators cannot rely on the family's participation in the Church rituals to bring sacramental wholeness. They must explore alternatives and paradigmatic shifts in formation, evaluation tools and expectations.

Parents

Roles Past and Present

In the 1970s and early 80s parents who brought their children for the sacraments were all about the same age. Their life experiences were similar. They had been raised on rules and regulations, safeguarded by the priests and religious. They had been taught that their responsibility in their child's faith formation was to take him or her to religious instruction (either through CCD classes or preferably the parochial school). Faith sharing in the home, assumed by the Church, had been abdicated by the parents. Catechizing the children for the sacramental celebrations was given priority in parishes. Religious educators contributed to this by focusing on child classroom formation and relegating parent meetings to *informational* nights. Since adult formation was virtually nonexistent, parents went about the business of secular life and left sacramental formation to the Church. Parent involvement was relegated to planning the home parties. The gap between sacrament performance and sacramental understanding widened, forcing the focus of the family to dealing with the external/outside the realm of sacramental rites. Their responsibility/involvement centered on the party/ dress – societal issues shaped by their commensurate lifestyle.[4]

By the late-80s, significant numbers of 3D Boomers were showing up in the pews. They had reached midlife and were seeking to reclaim their religious heritage. Most were motivated by a desire to give their children values and morals. Boomers express a sense of obligation to support some religious training, some religious upbringing of their children. For divorced and single parents, Mass and religion class attendance present a true balancing act, often leading to the neglect of one or both. Today, the ages of our parents at sacramental preparation meetings encompass both waves of Boomers.[5] The characteristics of their generation based on their life experiences as well as their sacramental experiences incline them to regard their own "theologies" as superior to the accounts of others, especially those viewed as a part of the institutional Church.[6] The conflict becomes even more intense when there is the underlying notion that since the parents were taught by nuns and religious, the current lay catechists and Directors of Religious Education are obviously wrong.

Parent Dreams and Desires

A random sampling of Cincinnati parishes shows that Baby Boomers comprise more than 95% of the parents who are bringing their children to Church to participate in the sacraments. They are Loyalists, Returnees and Dropouts. They all desire the same thing for their children: the best. They say they want a meaningful sacramental experience but most are unsure what that really means. Parents often operate out of emotional trappings wrapped around memories of what they think they remember from their childhood. They come with dreams based on these memories and expectations from their youth. For a large percentage, those dreams clash not just with the Director of Religious Education but with the reality of the sacrament. As Greeley points out, religious imaginations acquired early in life are difficult to give up, especially in a Baby Boomer society where differences continue to be an important factor in providing self-definition and social location.[7]

Parents who seek to recreate their sacramental experience for their children find little resemblance in the formation and celebrations of today. The sacramental language of ritual, symbol, and community is foreign to them because they were never exposed to it. They find the "things" that they equated with the sacraments have been changed or dropped completely. They feel threatened by the thought that what they learned was wrong and their faith foundation is shaken. "Why isn't there a scapular enrollment with First Holy Communion?" "Where are the arm bows and veils?" "Why must my child wait until high school for Confirmation? I was confirmed in third grade and it was good enough for me." "What do you mean us parents need to take the opportunity to reflect on the sacrament? I already got mine."

If sacramental economy is to survive, change is in order. The Church community as a whole must be evangelized with a Christ-centered sacramental understanding. The understanding must be clearly connected to everyday reality. Vatican II called for a renewed sacramental focus. Religion is for adults and yet their childlike sacramental understanding remains. The pastoral rush to bandage the sacramental wounds by requiring parents to attend adult education classes is a contradiction in terms. Restricting the reception of sacraments only to children whose parents have been forced to attend classes is neither pastoral nor effective. Boomers shun parishes whose spiritual growth is motivated by obligation rather than inspiration and which are insensitive to their needs. They either begrudgingly attend parent updating sessions remaining close-minded or simply choose to withdraw from the parish. These responses serve only to heighten the unrest of the faithful and plunge their sacramentality deeper into turmoil.

Reaching Out to Boomer Parents

McNeill pointed out that Boomers in the pews are seeking the 3Cs: commitment, community and connectedness. How is a parish committed to its congregation if the staff fails to understand the needs of Boomers? For Boomers a return to Church is a search for something stable in their lives. They equate stability with their childhood and the memories of their Church community. Their sacramental initiation was a part of their childhood. When they discover that what rooted their sacramental imagination is no longer emphasized or present in today's Church, they feel duped. The sacramental imagination seeks to preserve every last bit of wisdom and sensitivity that the past has to offer. It rejects efforts to link the past with the present only when the evidence is incontrovertible that a given artifact or custom of the past can no longer be harmonized with the present.[8] For some, the undoing of past myths feels like a betrayal of their religious heritage. Many respond with anger and leave again.

A large percentage choose to stay. Some remain loyal to their beliefs and dismiss current teachings as temporary insanity which will dissipate when the current pastor and/or Director of Religious Education leave. They issue a challenge in finding a response that is pastoral but does not abandon sacramental responsibility. Joseph Champlin refers to these people as "Marginal Catholics" and states that they must be responded to with pastoral wisdom which "challenges, not crushes."[9]

Midlife Introspection – Boomers and Church

Still, a good many Boomers seek new insight into the rich and living symbolism of the sacraments. Their midlife introspection has uncovered a courage to seek what they have long felt missing. Some had long ago abandoned sacramental teachings which they felt limiting in light of their experience. "When my baby died at birth without having been baptized, I realized I had to either give up my belief in limbo or my belief in a loving God. The inconsistency of my sacramentality and formation was glaring." Boomers at midlife are open to, although cautious about entering a conversion process, one which leads their sacramental imagination back to a root metaphor of Christ.

The 1994 *Catechism* states: "The purpose of the sacraments is to make people holy, build up the Body of Christ, and offer worship to God. The sacraments confer the grace that they signify if they are celebrated in faith. This sacramental grace is the grace of the Holy Spirit."[10] The task of the Church is to enable the faithful to fully experience the sacraments. If the faithful's sacramental imagination does not subscribe to this current theology, it will remain incomplete.

Baby Boomers seeking connectedness turn to religion hoping to find meaning in their lives. Religion is learned through worship, prayer, hymnody, and familiar narratives recounted at appointed times of the year, far more than it could be learned from a propositional theology, or certainly from any empirically testable claims of such a theology.[11] For the Catholic Baby Boomer religion is anchored by their sacramental rituals. However, rituals based on incomplete sacramentality become empty, void of their purpose. Empty rituals cannot aid one in finding connectedness. Thus, the boomer is forced to find spiritual nourishment elsewhere.

Worgul states that there is no anesthetic for the pain of surrendering old "first principles" and embracing new ones. Because "first principles" are unconscious, they are usually recognizable only when one tastes the anxiety of the middle time.[12] Baby Boomers are living in this middle time. They have experienced turmoil and crisis in all areas of life. The turmoil in their sacramental life is arising from the shift in "First Principles" as their sacramentality is challenged to move beyond their initiation experience to greater wholeness.

Redefining the Mission

Throughout Paul's letters to the early Christians, he teaches that for a people to be a community of God, church, then faith must be vital to and for its life. For Catholics, faith experienced through and ritualized in the sacraments should be life giving. The Baby Boomer generation is not the first to attempt to address their fragmented sacramentality in the quest for sacramental wholeness. But as seen in other realms, a Boomer presence creates new agendas and forces issues that otherwise may be overlooked. The Church must take responsibility for its false assumptions and lack of adequate provisions. It can no longer respond to its people as children, for they are well educated and will not tolerate condescension. The clergy, religious and lay educators are called to respond pastorally to the Returnees and Dropouts as well as to the Loyalists. They are called to remember that the mission of the Church is to: (1) support, console and reconcile; (2) offer a path to the transcendent through a cult which in turn fosters social identity; (3) sacralize the norms and values of the established society; (4) offer a prophetic critique of established order; (5) foster social and personal identity by communicating to people who they are and what they are; and (6) sustain individuals through maturation crises co-relational to age.[13] Clergy and religious educators need to be empathic to the grief process of Boomers as they abandon their old attitudes. Clergy and religious educators must be courageous and Spirit guided in examining their own attitudes.

Baby Boomers must also be called to take responsibility for their own faith development. To have assumed that the Church would remain stagnant yet alive with the Spirit is unrealistic. As they enter midlife, and seek introspection through the sacraments, they are called to remain open. For although they may feel caught in a sacramental crisis, it would be wise for Boomers and their Church to remember Greeley's words: *"Between experience and reason, between image and doctrine, between story and creed there will always be tension, but there will also be fruitful interaction."*[14]

The next chapter will look at responsive implications for faith formation of Baby Boomers and their families.

Assisting Adult Faith Development: Implications for Present and future Religious formation

In this chapter we will explore the need for a shifting of religious formation practices, moving from teachable moments to reachable times. By utilizing the suggestions of Joseph Champlin, Patrick Brennan, and combined operational strategies from the field, offered here are ten guidelines for sacramental formation with Baby Boomer families.

facing the Crisis

As stated in the preface, this work grows out of a love-hate relationship with the sacramental preparation of Baby Boomer families and a desire to better minister with them. Religious Education in the 1980s and early 1990s concentrated on the child as the primary candidate for the sacrament. Parent meetings consisted mainly of information rather than formation. Perhaps it was because parents of the time had been raised with the motto of pay, pray and keep quiet. The idea that the authority of Father/Sister or

even the Lay Director in regards to sacramental practices could be questioned was unspeakable. Perhaps
it was because Vatican II reforms were still relatively
new and few adults had been updated accordingly.
It seemed that most parents were so gratified that
someone else was taking responsibility for their
child's faith formation that they joyfully relinquished
the task and maintained an almost hands-off approach.

Since the late 1980s, parent meetings have been
anything but simple information socials. Many priests
and directors of religious education refer to these
gatherings as time spent in Purgatory. As external
peripheral demands which seem to contradict or have
little sacramental meaning become cries of outrage
among parents, a sense of community and harmony
are destroyed. "My child must wear a veil and carry
a rosary at First Communion – it shows her reverence." "I pay good money to send my child to a
Catholic school, why should he have to participate
in a confirmation retreat with those CCD kids?"

The sacramental crisis facing religious educators
and Baby Boomers explored earlier, is forcing a reinterpretation of shared traditions often causing argument and conflict among the faithful, the
theoreticians, and the practitioners. Solace may be
taken in the discovery that our Church is still constituted by significantly shared meanings. Those
shared meanings are still worth passing on but require different venues.

Catholic Baby Boomers are being challenged to
reframe or release their sacramental attitudes. It is
difficult to alter what has so long been a part of their
myth. Moreover, if their imaginative heritage is to be
subject to critical reflection, then so too must formal

instruction listen to the experience of the Spirit at work in the world.[1] For the religious educator it is easier to remain status quo by repeating old formulas, to comfort oneself with the community's familiar practices, rather than to risk trusting new responses to new conditions.

Ritualistic practices which do not emphasize sacramental wholeness do not portray a Church alive with the Spirit of Christ. A repetition of old formulas that do not connect one's life with the reality of Christ's presence will not be tolerated by a community alive with the Spirit. The character of the Baby Boomer generation, their diverse sacramental understandings and their spiritual quest, have altered the conditions for religious education. *The key in ministry with Boomers moves us from the traditional approach of seeing the child's faith education as priority to concentrating on adult formation that is a life-long learning process.*

Reachable Moments

Sacramental formation done during the early 80s was expressed as "teachable moments" in the life of the child. Identifying the great need to evangelize parents, current archdiocesan guidelines refer to this time as a "reachable moment" and consider the whole family as a candidate for the sacrament.[2] Systematic catechesis which isolates the child's faith formation from his or her family and the parish community is limited at best. Family formation done outside of the classroom and within the parish is being promoted and essential for success in the "passing on" of faith.

Sensitivity to the boomer family structure is imperative. The traditional Catholic family of mom, dad and child(ren) appears to be in the minority. Recently the National Catholic Educators Association noted that only 10% of American families have two live-in birth parents. In its place are blended families, single parents, divorced Catholics, mixed-faith marriages. Weekly religion class attendance requirements must take into account shared custody as well as school vacations and a multitude of other scheduling conflicts.

Ten Basics for Reaching Out to Boomer Families

Joseph Champlin's suggestions for dealing with "Marginal Catholics" coupled with ideas expressed by Patrick Brennan along with suggestions and practices expressed in surveys with other DREs yield some guidelines in ministering to Baby Boomers seeking sacraments for themselves and/or their children.

1. *Teach the ideal in relation to reality.* The fundamental role of religious formation is to teach the ideal in relation to reality. One cannot enforce faith beliefs but presenting the ideal should not be sacrificed. A scripture passage here would help – demonstrating Jesus' preaching ideal but accepting people as they are. This is crucial and perhaps the most destructive to the "people pleaser" minister. The art of ministry has often been defined as the ability to comfort the challenged and to challenge the comfortable. Returnees or Dropout Boomers seeking the sacraments for their children come with a strong sense of security in their sacramental imagination devel-

oped during their childhood experiences. They relate to the sacraments in the way they think they remember their own initial celebrations. Being told that their understanding is limited at best, plunges them into the murky waters of the whirlpool of the sacramental crisis. This forces them to make a choice: to remain with their stagnant fragmented ritual or to abandon their given heritage. The need for compromise must be examined in relation to the ideal and reality. In this ever-changing world, small compromises can make the difference between the perception of an uncaring church or a church that fosters the development of the sacramental imagination. Compromises can be made that may alter a specific requirement or program but not jeopardize the integrity of the sacrament. Both require a pastoral response but one which does not undermine the ideals. Conservative Loyalists are also challenged and question why their children are not being taught the "correct" theology. Sometimes they leave, seeking parishes with more traditional formation and celebrations for their children. The challenge for the religious educator is not in proving how wrong the Boomers are but how they are right and then enabling them to move beyond that entry point.

2. *Parents are faith models for their children.* Priests and DREs need to practice what they have long preached: parents are the foremost religious educators of their children. The role of educator takes on many dimensions and is not limited to a text or classroom, in fact the shared faith experience between parent and child is paramount to the succession of religious practices. Parental partici-

pation is the difference between program attendance and involved family faith formation, but the requirements must remain flexible and pastoral. The challenge of initiating a child into sacramental ritual cannot be deemed successful if he or she continues to be nurtured by a domestic Church attuned to a skewed theology. No matter how good religious education classes are, if they do not parallel what is being practiced in the home they are worthless ventures. Father Patrick J. Brennan has written several books on his ministry with Baby Boomers, in *Re-Imaging the Parish*, he cites master teacher and catechist Johannes Hofinger's critique of religious education, "sacraments were distributed or celebrated with no concern for perceived conversion; religious education efforts seemed too focused on children, to the exclusion of parental involvement."[3] Brennan also refers to George Gallup's suggestion to improve evangelization in mainline churches: ". . . stop educating children and start evangelizing families."[4]

Brennan demonstrates that statistics regarding regularly worshiping children, teens, and families are alarming low. The child-centered approach is mass-producing the non-practicing, cultural Catholic. If the message at home is that what is presented at school or CCD is not something lived by or practiced in the family, then we have created a religious education schizophrenia, thus separating religion from living in the real world. Realizing family evangelization and catechesis is a necessity. Family involvement must be mainstreamed into religious education. Since the lifestyles of the Baby Boomers are diverse, formation should also be diverse. Time for the Baby Boomer is their greatest commodity. They will revolt against meetings that appear without a purpose.

All Boomers – Loyalists, Returnees and Drop-outs – need opportunities to develop the tools to be faith-filled, faith-practicing models for their children. In order to be effective, they themselves must reexamine their own sacramentality.

Formational opportunities should be designed with the adult learner in mind. Patrick Brennan refers to Malcolm Knowles' adult learning praxis called andragogy.[5] It encompasses a coordinated system of intellect, feelings, somatic experiences, morality, relationships. I demonstrated in Chapter I that these areas are in direct relationship with the Baby Boomers' spiritual search. Brennan says that ". . . a bearing down on a need in any one piece of the system can lead to a discovery of the God of mystery present in questions, needs, and humanity."[6] These are the areas the Baby Boomers' misaligned sacramentality cannot address. However, the creative, sensitive catechist (minister) will design family/parent formation which are sensitive to these needs. The greatest motivation for Boomers is the welfare of their children. This motivation will serve well in getting the parents to attend a formational meeting. The challenge comes in presenting enlightening and effective material which will have far reaching effects on such a diverse population. Understanding the make up of the Boomers, their current sacramentality combined with good adult catechetical practices ensures greater success.

3. *Include the laity in formational sessions.* Boomers' distrust of authority has been well documented. Other Boomers sharing their experiences give the

sense of community desired by Boomers and authenticate what practitioners and theoreticians are promoting. Relationship with peers is vitally important to this generation. While Pastors and DREs ministering to Baby Boomers may be held in high esteem by their colleagues, they should keep in mind the old adage: one cannot be a prophet in one's own land. It is often necessary to separate the administrator of the rules from the sharer of faith. Peers sharing personal experiences seem to be most helpful to the Returnees. They don't feel like they're the only ones who took a vacation. For Dropouts, this can also be a connection for reentry. "Hey, the Church really does understand." Loyalists appreciate the value found within their community. This type of sacramental sharing speaks in direct relation to the 3Cs (community, connectedness, commitment) sought by Baby Boomers.

4. *Listen.* Baby Boomers want to be heard. The starting point is in finding what the depth of the Baby Boomer's sacramental understanding is and then meeting them there. Determining the entry level can be accomplished only by careful listening. Listening and challenging can help the Boomer to also discern between sacramental needs and secular desires. Returnees and Dropouts often lack the vocabulary to articulate their needs. While Loyalists may have the vocabulary, they are still often stuck between what they want for their children and what the Church prescribes for a sacramental life.

   Calling one's sacramental imagination into question is painful. It often results in a grieving process and that process can be shrouded in anger. Whenever possible, personal interaction should be invited. As one DRE stated, nothing quells hostility better than inviting the angry parent to a private meeting. They may still go away angrily but at least both will have had the opportunity to express their views and will feel they were heard.

Returnees and Dropouts are often struggling with high guilt because they left. Anger because there are so many changes they don't understand. And fear because the Church just doesn't feel the same and maybe there won't be room for them anymore. These Boomers need to be reassured that they still are welcome in the Church. The presence of Christ remains in the Church as well as in their lives.

The reminder of Christ's presence needs to be affirmed for the Loyalists as well. They need to be heard and reaffirmed where they are. Their growth still needs to be encouraged as well. For many who remained physically, their spiritual, sacramental journey has been on hold.

5. *Visible support of the pastor, parish staff and community.* Support and understanding of the pastoral team is crucial. No matter what Vatican II says about the priestliness of the laity, the pastor must be visibly present and supportive. Boomers were raised with the notion that "father knows best." He is still the administrator of the sacraments. How he reacts to the impact of Baby Boomer theologies will have far reaching effects. He may also find his own sacramentality in need of wholeness. Many parish staffs and catechists are composed of very faith-filled persons who are themselves grappling with a fragmented sacra-

mentality. Parish staffs need to be united in their sacramental perspectives. Pastors should consider opportunities for staffs to share and grow in their own sacramental understandings. Sacraments should not be further fragmented by relegating aspects to various offices or committees (i.e. Only the Youth Minister is involved in confirmation). The pastoral staff's unity should serve the entire parish community as a model by their own involvement in the sacramental life of the parish.

Clear-cut pastoral guidelines and expectations defined by the community, embraced by the parish staff (and school staff) and endorsed by the pastor will serve the religious educator and the Boomer in the pew. The RCIA model lends itself well as an example of parish involvement into the sacramental life of the candidate. Full parish support in formation and celebration can enable the Drop-ins and Returnees to gain a sense of support and community. Loyalists will feel secure in the participating embrace.

6. *Encourage parish registration, not church envelopes.* Parish registration as a requisite for the sacraments demonstrates a commitment. Basing the depth of one's commitment by the amount put in the collection basket, sends a different message. What does registration in a parish mean? What are the entitlements? How will registration at St. Luke's be better for them at St. Mary's? Can this parish best suit the needs of my family – spirituality just one among many? How does this parish reach out to families – of all types? While financial support of the parish is important, it should not preclude one's desire

to participate in the sacraments. Such a notion implies that sacraments can be purchased or that they are an entitlement of paying tuition. The Boomer generation is one of the most charitable groups of people in history, yet, they require value for their money. If they see an active church tending to the needs of its community, then weekly contributions and donations will be reflected. A wise person once said, "If the mission of the church controls the budget, then the funds will come in abundance. If the budget controls the mission, then the mission is doomed." Returnees and Dropouts have often proclaimed that one of the motivating factors for having left in the first place was, "All Father preached about was money." When the parish welcome wagon consists of the Mass schedule, current newsletter and a box of offertory envelopes, then revolving doors may as well be installed at all the entrances. Stewardship efforts focused on time and talent should surpass concentration on treasure. Being Christ for one another is the focal point of community, not creating cash reserves.

Boomer Loyalists will remain if their families are nurtured by a parish with a spiritual presence. Returnees are encouraged to stay if they are welcome and assured that their membership is important to the strength of the community not just as a financial commodity.

7. *Avoid making Mass attendance a requirement for the sacraments.* The Church encourages and desires that every member have a great love for the Eucharist and obliges the faithful to participate in Mass every Sunday and holy day of obligation; however, the mention of Mass attendance as a

requirement for Baptism or Confirmation is not found in Church documents.[7] *The Catholic Myth* finds that financial support of the Church and weekly attendance at Mass are two behaviors that traditionally were seen as the benchmarks of "good Catholic." Today, 88% think that one can be a good Catholic without contributing money regularly to Church, while 85% think a person can be a good Catholic without going to Church every Sunday.[8] Loyalists tend to be more forgiving of the church when pastors don't make the grade. But, here again, Returnee and Dropout Boomers speak loudly with their feet. If liturgies are not nourishing, they will remain absent. If good, safe child care is not provided, it will be sought elsewhere. If Mass is not 'family friendly,' then for Boomers, their children's classes will suffice for the community worship. Many Boomer families are time broke. They are often forced to make choices between two goods: Mass attendance and a family event. The Church must be cautious in mandating a coerced spirituality. Returnees and Dropouts will walk.

8. *Be sensitive to special requests.* An attempt to set all encompassing rules and policies is being short-sighted especially to the diverse lifestyle of Baby Boomers and their culture. Christ's compassion is missing when a single mother working two jobs to keep her family together is told that her children cannot participate in the sacraments because they missed too many classes last year. What is truly being said when a First Communion celebration cannot be altered to allow for hospitality to the non-Catholic parent? Does a community value a family's needs when entrance into

a program is denied because a parent had to work instead of attending an informational meeting? Because of the diverse Boomer lifestyles, flexibility is a need shared by all – Loyalists, Returnees and Dropouts. Sensitivity and flexibility will ultimately determine paradigmatic shifts in the structure and form of catechetics. Current measuring tools are no longer appropriate and therefore must be altered to concur with the shift.

9. *Delay, but never refuse, the sacraments.* Vatican directives are explicit about this. Champlin would say that a delay can be challenging or crushing depending on the approach and the reception. Delaying a child's reception of the sacrament because his or her parents have a limited sacramental imagination speaks to the ideal, but the reality may preclude a reachable moment and forever close the door for both adult and child. Clearly a need for family formation speaks here. This is especially relevant for the Dropouts. Slamming the door in the face of these Boomers may seal it shut forever.

   Loyalists and Returnees will simply seek out parishes which will sacramentalize their children without all the hoops. If a decision to delay is made, it must clearly be the choice of the family. Consultation, close and continuous communication, among the pastor, religious educator and parents is a must. It is imperative that the rationale for such a delay is clear and in agreement. The criteria for participation in the liturgical ritual must be outlined and appropriate from the beginning of the process.

10. *Keep the life-death-resurrection experience in focus.* Boomers are challenged to allow the death of their limited sacramental imagination even though it somehow sustained their connection to the Church. In its stead, Boomers must find a Church which invites them to enter a sacramental imagination resurrected with the Christ. Loyalist Boomers are more open to this process. They have witnessed first hand the evolution of the Church. Yet, their pain is heavy since this may be the first time they have had to address it personally. Returnees reenter cautiously. They knew (consciously or subconsciously) that they may be forced to let go of past notions and understandings, but their grief is strong. For some Returnees and Dropouts the death experience may be harsher, the resurrection experience unreachable. The very reason which inspired their return their attendance may have seemingly vaporized. Tending to their grief maybe all encompassing and the focus of much pastoral attention. The presence of the risen Christ guiding a Church fully alive with the Spirit must be within visible reach.

Religious educators faced with Boomers in sacramental formation also enter into a life-death-resurrection experience of their ministry and styles of religious formation. Failure to do this will allow for a repeat of our failed past. Boomers challenge catechesis to move from its period of stagnation[9] and become creative. Tom Walters in his workshops, "Questions on the Hopeful Horizons," challenges catechetical leaders to be pioneers seeking new ways to meet the needs of today's faithful. Endless studies have demonstrated the failure of current methods. Yet the process continues because so much energy is already invested. There is pain in letting go and resurrection is uncertain, but only a resurrection will ensure a continued life of the Sacramental Church.

Traditionally, the Church has viewed itself as a "messy" faith family. The Church of today is like it was in the beginning, a community of different disciples, of saints and sinners, of committed and uncommitted, of hot, lukewarm and cold followers. Nowhere is this diversity more explicit than with Baby Boomers. No less has their impact been felt than in today's sacramental formation and celebration. Sacramental formation today must embrace the whole family as the candidate. It is a "messy" task, but if the Catholic faith is to remain vital and alive, then every opportunity must be secured to keep the sacraments from becoming empty rituals.[10]

The key words to keep in mind are family-focused and diverse. Baby Boomers demand both. If parishes are to survive today, they must be both tolerant and creative in their response, expectations and evaluation tools. What does living a sacramental life look like? Are we as a community of Church achieving it? Do our current formation practices truly tend to the needs of those in the pews? What must change? These questions must be addressed by the faithful, theoreticians and practitioners alike.

This chapter offered some excellent theories on preparing and programming for Baby Boomers. Our next section will summarize this work and demonstrate two programs created and implemented with the Baby Boomer family in mind.

Chapter Five

Summation and Conclusion: Reaction and Actions Taken

The purpose in the preceding chapters has been to enable the Catholic practitioners and theoreticians to gain valuable insights into the diversity of the Baby Boomer generation's relationship with the sacraments. Most Catholics are rooted to the Church by their sacramental relationship. This concluding chapter contains four parts: summations of key points; additional observations; a brief review of two programs I developed and implemented based on this research; and a final thought.

Summary

This work began with an attempt to define Baby Boomers. Although ministers to Boomers must exercise caution to avoid stereotyping and making sweeping generalizations, some specific trends can be delineated. Plotting the yearly birth rates displayed a two-wave dynamic. A review of the secular and religious historical events during their youth and young adulthood has proven to be key in understanding and ministering to Baby Boomers. Most Boomers today have been identified as 3D (delayed marriage, deferred childbearing, high divorce rates) looking for the 3Cs (community, connections, commitment). Three basic Boomer spiritualities have been theoretically defined, discovered in the pews and highlighted. Catholic Boomers relate to the Church of their parents as Loyalists, Returnees, Dropouts and all shades in between.

An overview of sacraments as ritual, sign and symbol, community and narrative was briefly discussed. The sacramental imagination as key to one's ability to create meeting places with God was found to be the glue which has kept Catholics Catholic. The works of Andrew Greeley, Alex Garcia-Rivera, Brennan Hill and George Worgul were used to build the foundation for this premise. Support for these theories/theologies was found throughout interviews and discussions with Boomers. The chaos of the times both internally and externally was illuminated as a major catalyst for the fragmented sacramentality among many Boomers today. Three identifiable fragmented attitudes have resulted: (1) Rules and Rubrics, (2) Magic, and (3) Me and Thee. A further fragmentation has resulted in the secularization of the sacraments.

The sacramental crisis, derived from a collision of fragmented sacramentalities and a quest for sacramental wholeness, was exposed. Some espouse a need to protect the sacredness of the sacraments from the secularness of the Baby Boomers. It has been proven that Boomers will commit, connect and participate in community if they feel that the Church is committed to keeping Christ's presence in the real world, the parish offers a community to which they can relate, and they are enabled to connect the sacraments and real life in a wholistic way.

The keys to religious formation with Baby Boomers were outlined. These demonstrated the necessity for a paradigmatic shift from child formation to family formation. Parental involvement and lifelong spiritual formation are key to the success of sacramental preparation and wholeness. Ten basics for designing and implementing programs were enumerated.

Additional Observations

Most of us in the field have fully embraced Vatican II, feeling liberated and empowered. But in sacrament discussions with many Boomers, references to Vatican II teachings are often met with open hostility or blank stares. Why? The religious life cycle of most Americans includes a vacation from organized religion between late teens and early to mid-thirties. Plotting the ages of Boomers on a graph shows that the majority of First Wave Boomers had already "completed" their formation when Vatican II occurred (see plate 4). The effects of Vatican II for most First Wave Boomers are viewed as a dismantling or doing away with their foundational formation. Most Second Wave Boomers were catechized for the sacraments immediately following the Council but prior to the implementation of its teachings as catechetical tools. Thus, Vatican II was disseminated while most of them were on vacation. While adhering to the mandates of Vatican II, practitioners must remember that most Boomers have little knowledge or concern about its teachings. Therefore, as discouraging as this may be, it is imperative that this, too, is considered when looking for a starting point in family formation and sacramental preparation.

The sacramental imagination of many Boomers has been skewed by religious formation and sacrificed for technological advancement. Boomers are more highly educated than their parents, twice as many have attained college degrees. Higher education not only opened their lives but has had a great impact on the narrowing of the imagination. Technical courses and career-oriented classes became the focus of universities. The quest for the real and proven absorbed their studies. Philosophical and classical exploits were relegated as general education requirements to suffer through on the way to obtaining a degree and ticket to a better career. The idea of magic and imagination became irrelevant and hence discarded. Now Boomers are sensing a contradiction within by desiring the magic and mystery of a faith held by belief as opposed to their need for scientific proof. Unlike earlier generations, opportunities for the development of an imagination have been abandoned. (Boomers who are insistent on structuring their children's free time with organized activity may be further bankrupting the gift of imagination).

Boomers' multi-layered beliefs and practices offer a rich melding of traditions and existential concerns which can be empowering. Their movement to overcome Western culture's dualistic stances on humanity and the environment has caused a renewed appreciation of the core teachings of our faith. They are the generation which started the ecological movement. They are willing to be more generous with time, talent and treasure if it is a matter to which they can commit. When invited to share their gifts, Boomers bring a wealth of skills and creativity.

Children and time are considered their most prized possessions. Boomers seek out others who believe this as well. If Baby Boomers are to be reached and their sacramental imagination recreated to wholeness, then the Church must reach out responsibly to welcome them. While focusing on child formation may seem to play to the values of the Baby Boomer, it does not encourage life long formation nor enable parents to assume a responsible role in the child's faith education. Such a course continues to play to the externals that act as barriers to an internal faith and sacramental imagination. It perpetuates the notion that faith formation is a graded course of study with its outcome ritualized by a sacramental celebration. Productive gatherings allow parents to discuss and experience faith on an adult level while at the same time empowering them to discuss and experience sacraments with their children.

Ministering to Baby Boomers has caused many of my colleagues to reevaluate their vocation, myself included. This generation of parents is far different from their seemingly docile predecessors. Boomers are used to living in crisis and demanding what they want. Their number has kept them at the center of media attention. Commercials and products are targeted specifically with the boomer in mind. During the late 60s and early 70s they learned how to protest. They were taught that they could be anything they wanted and if they worked hard enough (or protested strongly enough) they could have whatever they desired. Many Boomers, who have these characteristics, coupled with a fragmented theological understanding of the sacraments, have ignited many a Director of Religious Education's burnout. Some DREs write off Boomers and wait in joyful hope of generations to come. But we cannot fragment our ministry if we are preaching wholeness. We are challenged to respond creatively and responsibly in meeting the needs and demands of Baby Boomers.

Two Successful Programs

When I began my tenure as a Director of Religious Education I came with enthusiasm and naivete. After my first baptism by fire, I felt I had three choices: resign, renounce my calling or refocus my understanding and energy. I chose the third (although there are many days I considered the other two). I had to scrap all my preconceived notions about the people in the pews and my programs and truly begin listening to what they were saying. I found my own beliefs challenged. Tried and true programs of the past were trying and not necessarily true. I began looking at some alternative models and decided to take the leap.

LLOFT

Our CCD program for students preschool through 8th grade grew from 450 students to 700+ in three years. Juggling work schedules, activities and Mass attendance with CCD times was a frustration for parents, children and catechists alike. The weekly structure of student classes appeared limited and limiting to most families, especially the Boomers. Such large classes were not conducive to building community. For many the weekly structure of Sunday morning or Wednesday evening was not prime learning time. The competition between family time, Mass time and other activities often forced parents to make choices between several "goods." The sharing of a classroom with other grades and/or day school students limited the room arrangement and often gave the sense that the CCD students were intruders.

After two years of research, creative dreaming and supportive encouragement, I implemented a pilot program entitled LLOFT – Living and Learning Our Faith Together.[1]

LLOFT has four components: a two-week systematic catechesis for students in grades one through eight (thirty-five hours); four liturgically based family gatherings; parental/family instruction and reinforcement of the text materials; and family sacramental formation. The two-week summer classes for the students include lessons, prayer services, crafts, videos, music, liturgy and community building. Parents are encouraged to join in whenever possible. (We often set up extra chairs during our daily closing prayer services.) Parents organize snacks, phone calling and secretarial duties.

Families accept the responsibility for the Family Gatherings. The goals of the gatherings are to be formational and community building. They've included the sharing of traditions, talents and creativity. Students have been treated to storytellers. Parents have been affirmed in their roles and encouraged to find Christ's presence within the doldrums of parenting. Forty families carved out a sense of community in a parish of twenty-four hundred families.

Student, parent and teacher evaluations were more like testimonials. All the teachers re-upped. Only one family failed to complete the components. All eligible families enrolled again for the next year. As one Boomer parent said, this program offers opportunities for prayer, liturgy and learning for the whole family.

Future plans included adding the following components: monthly Family Gatherings open to the whole parish and weekly Liturgy of the Word for Children.[2] These appeal to Boomers because they speak most closely to what they value: their time and their children. Quality is imperative and I finally learned that small steps are often better (and certainly safer) than giant leaps. Empowering people to take ownership and responsibility is a key to success.

Family Focused Sacrament Formation

The second program, which is actually a spin off from LLOFT, is a new Family Focused Formation program for Eucharist. (One was also developed for Reconciliation formation, but not included here.) LLOFT families are required to participate, but we also open up the program for all families whose child(ren) are preparing for the sacrament. With the help of our Adult Education Minister the adult program was developed to reach parents, especially Baby Boomers, whose sacramentality was in need of reshaping or renewal. Each student session paralleled the adult themes, yet was at the students' level of understanding. Only the adult themes and intentions for Eucharist are explored here. Complete outlines of the four adult and student sessions are included in the appendix.

The first session looks at the ritual and the changes over the years. For the adults it is intended to identify the fragmented theologies currently held by many parents. It enables them to identify their sense of fear and confusion over the changes which have taken place since their reception as children. They are affirmed yet challenged to grow.

The second session focuses on the presence of the risen Christ. As outlined earlier, the re-imagining of the root metaphor is imperative to our sacramentality. Moving from disconnected actions to a celebration of real presence enables one to make connections from secular reality to spiritual reality. The presentation and small group discussion free the limited notion of confining Christ only to the sacraments.

The horizontal nature of the sacrament is developed in the third session. Participants are encouraged to find Eucharist in the cracks of their lives. Finding the Christ within, identifying Christ in and through others, and sharing in the life-giving presence of Christ challenges the adults to move from a me and thee relationship into one of community.

The fourth session is designed to speak to the imagination. A video, *The Potter*, a guided imagery and a small group discussion focusing on Romans 9:20-21, lead to the discovery of the transforming nature of the Eucharist. It is an exercise in reestablishing a connection to the Sacramental Imagination.

Evaluations have included references to enlightenment from every session. Those who were unable to attend all four sessions expressed sadness and suggested that we videotape the sessions and make them available to those absent. Most stated that they feel prepared to enter into the sacrament in a new way and are open to being transformed.

Everyone commented on the importance of the family formation and activities. They felt that their own sacramental understanding has been enhanced. They share a sense of enablement and encouragement in their roles as their children's primary religious educators.

A Final (but Unending) Thought

My experience throughout this venture kept drawing me back to a HELP letter I received several years ago during a Christ Renews His Parish weekend. It contains a quotation from Robert Fulgrum which underlies my sacramental essence as Baby Boomer, Family Life Minister, Director of Religious Education and Catholic. For me, it has served as a focal point for my work, life, faith, and sacramentality. I offer Fulgrum's words now to the reader for reflection as he or she continues the journey of faith among Baby Boomers.

I believe that imagination is stronger than knowledge –
that myth is more potent than history.
I believe that dreams are more powerful than facts –
that hope always triumphs over experience –
that laughter is the only cure for grief.
And I believe that love
is stronger than death.

Bibliography

Works Cited

"Baby Boomers Have Created Their Own Religious Shock Wave," *PRRC Emerging Trends* Feb. 1994: 16.

Bellah, Robert N., et al. *Habits of the Heart.* New York: Harper & Row, 1985.

Bellah, Robert N., et al. *The Good Society.* New York: First Vintage Books Edition, 1992.

Brennan, Patrick J. *Re-Imagining Parish.* New York: Crossroad 1993.

Champlin, Joseph M. *The Marginal Catholic: Challenge, Don't Crush.* Notre Dame: Ave Maria Press, 1989.

Collins, Dr. Gary R. & Dr. Timothy E. Clinton. *Baby Boomer Blues.* Dallas: Word Publishing, 1992.

Dues, Greg. *Catholic Customs & Traditions.* Mystic: Twenty-Third Publications, revised 1992.

Garcia-Rivera, Alex. "Sacraments: Enter the World of God's Imagination." *U.S. Catholic* Jan. 1994: 6-12.

Greeley, Andrew M. *The Catholic Myth.* New York: Collier Books, 1990.

Hill, Brennan. *Rediscovering the Sacraments.* New York: Sadlier, 1982.

Hill, Brennan and William Madges. *The Catechism Highlights and Commentary.* Mystic: Twenty-Third Publications, 1994.

McNeill, Kirk. *Going for the Baby Boomers: A Workbook.* Nashville: MFG Publishing, 1990.

Roof, Wade Clark. *A Generation of Seekers.* San Francisco: Harper, 1993.

Whalen, William J. *How Different Christian Churches Celebrate the Sacraments.* Clarian Publications, 1980.

Worgul, George S. *From Magic to Metaphor.* New York: Paulist Press, 1980.

Works Consulted

Bausch, William J. *Ministry Traditions, Tensions, Transitions.* Mystic: Twenty-Third Publications, 1982.

Becker, Verne. "A Church for Bored Boomers." *Christianity Today* Oct. 1989: 29, 25.

Berkley, James. "The Marketing of a Boomer Church." *Christianity Today* Feb. 11, 1991: 34-36.

Boys, Mary C. *Educating in Faith.* San Francisco: Harper & Row, 1989.

Brennan, Patrick J. *The Evangelizing Parish.* Texas: Tabor, 1987.

Brennan, Patrick J. *Parishes That Excel.* New York: Crossroad, 1992.

Brennan, Patrick J. *The Reconciling Parish.* Texas: Tabor, 1990.

Champlin, Joseph M. "Welcoming Marginal Catholics." *Church* Spring 1989: 3-8.

DeGidio, Sandra, O.S.M. "First Communion: A Parish Event." *Catholic Update* Feb. 1984.

DeGidio, Sandra. *Sacraments Alive.* Mystic: Twenty-Third Publications, 1991.

Engel, James F. "We Are the World." *Christianity Today* Sept. 24, 1990: 32-34.

Gelpi, Donald L., S.J. *Beyond Individualism.* Notre Dame: Notre Dame Press, 1989.

Hater, Robert J. *News That Is Good.* Notre Dame: Ave Maria Press, 1990.

Martos, Joseph, PhD. *The Sacraments: Seven Stories of Growth.* Liguori: Liguori, 1989.

McCord, H. Richard. "Families Today: Many Faces, Many Voices." *The Catholic World* July/August 1993:1 48-153.

Moran, Gabriel. *Religious Education Development: Images for the Future.* Minneapolis: Winston Press, Inc., 1983.

New American Bible. New York: Catholic Book Publishing Co., 1970.

O'Brien, David J. "Catholic Evangelization and American Culture." *U.S. Catholic Historian* Spring 1993:49-59.

Ostling, Richard N. "The Church Search." *Time* 4 April, 1993: 44+.

Pedersen, Mary Miller. "The Family: Symbol of God's Covenant Love." *The Catholic World* July/August 1993: 148-153.

Pippert, Wesley G. "A Generation Warms to Religion." *Christianity Today* 6 Oct. 1989: 33: 22-3.

Richstatter, Thomas, O.F.M. "The Sacrament of the Eucharist." *Catholic Update* Sept. 1992.

Richstatter, Thomas, O.F.M. "Sacraments: It All Starts with Jesus." Catholic *Update* Aug. 1993.

Rolheiser, Ronald. *Spirituality for a Restless Culture.* Mystic: Twenty-Third Publications, 1991.

Roof, Velma C. "Social Systems and Family Life." *The Catholic World* July/August 1993: 148-153.

Roof, Wade Clark. "The Four Spiritual Styles of Baby Boomers." *USA Weekend* Mar. 19-21, 1993: 4-6.

(The) Sacrament of Eucharist, Archdiocesan Religious Education Office, Archdiocese of Cincinnati, 1992.

Thomas, David M. "What Every Family Needs: A Good Theology." *The Catholic World* July/August 1993: 148-153.

Turpin, Joanne. "The Sacramentals, Embracing God Through Creation." *Catholic Update* July 1993.

Veverka, Fayette Breaux. "Re-imaging Catholic Identity: Toward an Analogical Paradigm of Religious Education." *USA: The Religious Education Association* 1993: 238-254.

Walters, Tom. *Questions on the Hope Filled Horizon.* Parish Coordinators/Directors of Religous Education Oct. 1993:2-6.

Westly, Dick. *Redemptive Intimacy: A New Perspective for the Journey to Adult Faith.* Mystic: Twenty-Third Publications, 1991.

Whitehead, Evelyn Eaton and James D. *Community of Faith: Crafting Christian Communities Today.* Mystic: Twenty-Third Publications, 1992.

Workshops/Lectures

which continued to verify my theory and give more insights into the "crisis." (participated and/or facilitated).

Alternative Models of Religious Education – Rationale, Judith Dunlap – (presenter). Principals' Institute/ Catechetical Leader's Day, Aug. 1993. Diocese of Toledo (participant).

Alternative Models of Religious Education – LLOFT Model. Principals' Institute/Catechetical Leader's Day, Aug. 1993. Diocese of Toledo (presenter).

Alternative Models of Religious Education – LLOFT Model. National Conference of Catechetical Leaders, April, 1994 (presenter).

Preparation for First Communion: In the Begnning There Were (and Still Are) the Parents. Religious Education Congress, Sept. 1993. Archdiocese of Cincinnati (presenter).

Ohio Catholic Education Association Convention, Sept. 30- Oct. 1, 1993. Elements of a Family Spirituality Confirmation/RCIA Model Teachers, Evangelizers and Family (participant).

Questions on the Hopeful Horizon. Dr. Tom Walters (presenter). Principals' Institute/Catechetical Leader's Day, Aug. 1993. Diocese of Toledo (participant).

Reaching Out to the Baby Boomers: A Workshop for Enhancing Evangelization facilitated by Kirk McNeill. Continuing Ministerial Education Program, Athenaeum of Ohio, March, 1993 (participant).

Appendix
■ ■ ■ ■ ■

Family Focused Preparation:
First Eucharist

Outlines and Handouts

SESSION I: History and Theology of the Eucharist

Parents

7:00 PM   Welcome and Introduction
          Opening Prayer

7:05   Focusing Exercise
          Eucharist has been changing since the
          time of Jesus. This illustrates the fact that
          the Holy Spirit is always with us. Leading
          us to be friends in Christ. It is important
          to remember that although our celebra-
          tions may have changed dramatically
          since we were children, there were saints
          then and there are saints today.

          Share with your neighbor your response
          to the following:
          1) Recall your first experience of Eucha-
          rist, whether it was a separate First Com-
          munion Mass, a Sunday Mass, or some
          other occasion.
          2) Recall and share your most recent ex-
          perience. Contrast it to your first.

7:15   Presentation – Changes in the Liturgy (*Worshipping Wilma* video/filmstrip may be used)

7:40   Small Group Reflection
Divide parents into groups of 6-10, invite them to discuss:
(1) What aspect of the history of Eucharist interested you most? Did the historical perspective help you understand the Eucharist better?
(2) Do you feel like Wilma (confused) sometimes? How would you help Wilma? What would help you?

8:05   Large Group Comments
(On posted newsprint or chalkboard, write down their comments)

8:20   Homework Assignment (handout)

8:25   Closing Prayer

8:30   Dismissal

Materials: Video/filmstrip: *Worshipping Wilma* (Teleketics), TV, VCR, name tags, sign in sheets, pens, newsprint. Handouts: focusing questions, homework.

Students

7:00   Students make name tags

7:05   Welcome, introduction of catechist (recommend one adult for every ten students)

7:10   Icebreaker – "Find Someone Who" Bingo (handout). Directions: Use each person only once (if numbers permit). Give the first one done a little prize.

7:25	Introduction to media Video: *In My Father's House*
7:50	Small Group Discussion of the movie (What did you like? How was the Father's house different from yours? The same?, etc.).
8:00	Activities – *Graces* (handout) Directions: Talk about saying grace. Why is it important. Share what you and your family say (and/or do) at meal times.

Distribute the Grace sheets. Review and discuss the various graces included. Point out to the students that there are lines at the bottom of the page. They can write their own grace (either one they say or create a new one) to share with the family.

Love Soup (handout)
Directions: Explain to the children that often times we refer to Eucharist as The Last Supper. It was a meal Jesus shared with his friends. He gave us his love, and asks us to share his peace with everyone.

Now explain to the children that we are creating a soup to feed the world. We are trying to get Jesus' message to everyone. Ask the children, "What are some of the things we might include in our soup (i.e. love, peace, sharing, etc.)"

Give each child a slip of paper or a 3"x5" index card, placing the card in a vertical position, have the children write "LOVE SOUP" across the top. Then have them list various items (love, peace, helpfulness, etc.)

When finished, distribute the "pots" (pattern included). Instruct the children to write their name on their pot. Place their *recipe* in their pot. Tape back (see pattern). Remind children to take home their Graces and Pots to share with their families.

8:25   Closing Prayer – sung *Song of the Body of Christ*

8:30   Dismissal

Materials: Video/filmstrip: *In My Father's House* (Franciscan Communications), TV, VCR, name tags, music and tape recorder, tape. Handouts: Ice Breaker, Graces, Pots, Recipe Cards.

SESSION I: Handouts

Homework

Family Reflection: Jesus is the Light of the World

Before the next Session:

1. Read and reflect on Matthew 5:3-16.

2. Darken the room.
   Light a candle in the dark and discuss how much more you can do in the light.
   Discuss the warmth of the light.

3. Talk about Christ as the light of the World and his telling us we should be light. Discuss how we can be light for one another.

4. Help you child decorate a candle for his/her First Communion party.

After Mass this weekend:

1. Talk about the day's scripture stories.
2. Share some ideas as to what your family can do to live out the Gospel message.
3. Spend some time in the sanctuary after Mass. Relate how different the physical appearance of the church is today compared to the way it was when you were your child's age.

(Based on suggestions contained in the recommended guidelines of the Archdiocese of Cincinnati sacramental packets).

Session I – (Students)

FIND
SOMEONE
WHO . . . **and have them sign their name**

1. Wasn't born in this state _____

2. Moved within the past 2 years _____

3. Has a dog _____

4. Likes to eat watermelon _____

5. Knows how to rollerblade _____

6. Has blue eyes _____

7. Has been to a circus _____

8. Likes to eat broccoli _____

9. Has ridden in a boat _____

10. Visited a foreign country _____

11. Has a ribbon in her hair _____

12. Is wearing Reeboks™ _____

13. Whose favorite color is orange _____

14. Wears glasses _____

15. Watches "Saved by the Bell" _____

Use each person only once. The first to gather all 15 signatures wins a prize.

Session I – (Students)

GRACES

Beginning to Eat

With the first bite,
I promise to practice
loving kindness.
With the second,
I promise to help others.
With the third,
I promise to be happy
for others.
With the fourth,
I promise to follow
the way of Jesus.

Bless our hearts

• that we may hear in the
• breaking of bread
• what you call us to be

Beloved Lord
   Almighty God
Make me your own
   heal my body,
   and soul . . . . amen

God to enfold me, God to surround me,
God in my speaking, God in my thinking.
God in my sleeping, God in my waking,
God in my watching, God in my hoping.
God in my life, God in my lips,
God in my soul, God in my heart,
God in my playing, God in my slumber.
God in my ever-living soul,
God in my serenity. (Author unknown)

Eat your food with joy and
drink with happiness,
Knowing that
God blesses you
Greatly.

God is Great,
God is Good.
And we Thank
God for our Food.

Session I – (Students)

POT for LOVE SOUP

Transfer pattern onto black (or choice of color) construction paper. It is best to have the "pots" all cut out and prepared for the children ahead of time. Or make copies of the "Canned Soup"

SESSION II:
Eucharist: Presence of the Risen Christ

Parents

7:00 PM	Welcome and Introductions Opening Prayer (song: Song of the Body of Christ)
7:15	Large Group: Share comments from last week, responses to last week's family reflection
7:25	Presentation (or video on *Eucharist as the Presence of the Risen Christ*)
8:00	Small Group Reflection In your own personal faith life, where have you best experienced the presence of Christ? In Eucharist we receive Jesus and try to model our lives after Him. How might this affect our attitudes toward other people?
8:20	Large Group Comments (Write their comments on newsprint)
8:25	Homework Assignment (handout)
8:30	Closing Prayer and Dismissal
Materials:	video: *Jesus* (Tabor, 1983), *Exploring the Faith: Practical Theology for Students* (Tape 5, CTNA, 1990), or *Incarnation* (Corpus Video, 1993). TV, VCR, name tags, sign-in sheet, pens, newsprint, handouts, music and cassette player.

Students

7:00	Students make name tags
7:05	Welcome, introduction of catechists

7:10   Icebreaker – *Eucharist Words* (handout)
        Directions: Talk about the many ways we
        make "eucharist" happen for others, i.e.
        showing love, sharing, caring for the poor.

        Explain to the children that they need to
        find a partner and work together to make
        words out of the letters from Eucharist
        (i.e.: listen, laugh, smile, think).

        Distribute *"Eucharist"* sheets and pencils.
        Display the completed sheets around the
        room.

7:25   Introduction to media
        Video: *Martin the Cobbler*

7:40   Small Group discussion on the video

7:50   Activity: *Eucharist Banner*

        Directions: Explain to the children that
        Jesus is always with us. He is present
        right here in this very room and with them
        every minute of every day. Eucharist is a
        celebration of Jesus' presence. Distribute
        "bread" sheets and pencils. Review direc-
        tions with them, tell them to write the
        words, in order on the lines. Distribute
        "chalice" sheets and pencils. Review di-
        rections with the children.

        Make sure each group has a box of cray-
        ons or markers. Have the children color
        both the bread and chalice. Have them
        cut out the chalice, bread and their
        prayer.

        Distribute the title sheets (Eucharist Cele-
        brates the Presence of Jesus). Allow them
        to color or decorate their "title sheet."

Distribute the large pieces of construction paper, scissors and glue sticks. Explain to the children that they are to arrange their chalice, bread, prayer and title on the construction paper to make a banner for their family to share.

8:25   Closing Prayer – sung *Song of the Body of Christ*

8:30   Dismissal

Materials: Video: *Martin the Cobbler* (Billy Budd, 1976). TV, VCR, name tags, sign-in sheet, handouts, large sheets of construction paper, scissors, glue sticks, crayons, music tape and recorder.

SESSION II: Handouts

Homework

Family Reflection: Jesus tells us He is present when we celebrate Eucharist.

During the week:

1. Read and reflect on Mark 14:22-25

2. Explain that on the night before He died, Jesus had a meal with his friends. At the meal, he changed bread and wine into his body and blood.

3. Explain that Jesus asked his followers to do this so that, when we share his body and blood, we receive the help we need to follow Jesus.

4. Ask your child to explain his/her banner made tonight. Use your child's prayer at dinner time this week.

After Mass this weekend:

1. Talk about the day's scripture stories.

2. Share some ideas as to what your family can do to live out the Gospel message.

3. Take your child to the baptismal font. While there, share with him/her the story of his/her baptism (where it was, what he or she wore, who was there, etc).

4. Share any pictures you might have of your child's baptism. Help your child write a letter to his/her godparents.

(Based on suggestions contained in the recommended guidelines of the Archdiocese of Cincinnati sacramental packets.)

Session II – (Students)

Eucharist Words

_____E_____

_____U_____

_____C_____

_____H_____

_____A_____

_____R_____

_____I_____

_____S_____

_____T_____

Then He Took the Cup and, After Thanking God,
He Give It to Them with the Words,
"Drink This, All of You . . ."
Matthew 26:27

Unscramble these
words.

Some are spelled
sideways, some
are spelled
up and down.

Color the picture!

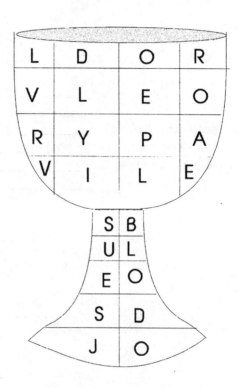

Prayer: Write a prayer to our Lord using all or most of the
words above.

_____

_____

_____

> While they were eating,
> Jesus took a piece of bread
> gave it to his disciples with these words,
> "Take and eat it, this is my body."
> Matthew 26:26.

Unscramble these
words. They are
spelled sideways.

_____
_____
_____
_____
_____
_____

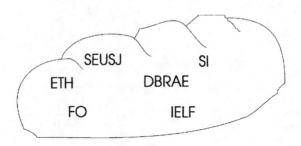

SEUSJ   SI

ETH   DBRAE

FO   IELF

EUCHARIST

CELEBRATES THE

PRESENCE OF JESUS

SESSION III:
Real Presence of Christ: Eucharist, Family, Community, World

Parents

7:00	Welcome and Introductions Opening Prayer (song: *Song of the Body of Christ*)
7:15	Large Group: Share responses to last week's family reflection
7:25	Real Presence of Christ: Eucharist, Family, Community, World – personal witness from member of the parish or Video: *A Gift for Life.*
8:15	Small Group Reflection (divide into groups, 6-8) Have each group address one of the following:

Group 1: For us the Eucharist is both comfort and challenge, it involves not only "Jesus and me" but also "The Christ in All."

Group 2: To be a eucharistic people means to be a people living out an essential gratitude for the presence of the Christ in our lives.

Group 3: When we say, "Do this in memory of me," THIS involves Jesus' life, death and resurrection.

Questions: What do I think or feel about this statement?

What might I do in response?

How might we as a family respond to this or express our understanding of this by the way we live?

8:25	Large Group comments and Closing Prayer
8:30	Dismissal
Materials:	Video: *A Gift for Life*, (Twenty-Third Publications, 1986). TV, VCR, Cords, name tags, sign-in sheet, pens, newsprint, handouts, music and recorder.

Students

7:00	Students make name tags
7:05	Welcome and Introductions Opening Prayer
7:10	Icebreaker – hearts (handouts)

Directions: When each child arrives, they are to receive a half-heart. They are to decorate it any way they wish. Instruct them to make sure that they write their name on one side.

After they are finished, instruct them to sit in a circle.

Tell them that Jesus holds each of us closely in his heart, just as we are to hold him in our hearts. When we share Jesus' love with others, we share a part of our heart. For tonight and for the rest of the time that they will be preparing for First Eucharist, they will have a special prayer partner. Someone who also holds Jesus in his/her heart and is looking forward to the day that they can share Jesus in a new way. Explain to the children that they need to find the person who has the other side of their heart. It maybe someone they have known for a long time, or someone they are just meeting. It maybe someone who is their best friend or maybe someone they don't know very well. To Jesus, there are no strangers or people he doesn't already love.

Give them time now to find the person who has the other side of their heart. Instruct them to sit by that person.

Once everyone has found his/her person: each student is to exchange their side of the heart with their partner. Ask them to share with their partner why they decorated their half the way they did. Also share with them something about themselves (i.e. family members, school, when they will be celebrating communion).

7:25   Introduction to media (make sure to explain that there are some sad parts to the video). Video: *Grandma's Bread*.

7:50   Small Group reflection

8:00   Activity – Christ Silhouettes (handout)

Directions: Discuss how each of us is united by baptism and the Eucharist, share his or her life and is called to help make Christ present in our worldly actions. Talk about who/what reminds you of Christ's loving presence (i.e. Grandma from the movie, family members, flowers). Distribute white sheets of paper with the rectangle to the students (handout). Instruct them to draw, using crayons or markers, pictures of everyone and everything that is "Christ" to them. Tell them to draw the pictures close together and keep inside the square. When they are finished give each one of the construction paper sheets. (pattern) Fold the sheet in half with the markings on the outside. Instruct them to cut along the dark lines. When they have finished cutting, instruct them to open the sheet and see whose silhouette they have (Jesus Christ). Have the students then glue their Christ silhouette over their picture.

Next glue the caption "CHRIST IS IN US AS WE ARE IN HIM" on the top or bottom of their picture.

Remind them to take these home and explain their picture to their family.

8:25   Closing Prayer (song: *Song of the Body of Christ*). Signing is most effective.

8:30   Dismissal
Materials: Video: *Grandma's Bread* (Franciscan Communications, Los Angeles, #7152). TV, VCR, name tags, hearts, markers and crayons, glue sticks, scissors, white paper, Christ silhouettes, music tape and recorder.

SESSION III: Handouts

Homework

Family Reflection: Jesus tells us He is present when we celebrate Eucharist, in what other ways this week has Jesus been present to us.

During the week:

1. Read and reflect on Mark 14:32-16.

2. Recall that Jesus came to show us how to live and explain that Jesus gave us everything, even his life.

3. Explain that Jesus came with a new life after his death. You might want to use the analogy of a caterpillar spinning a cocoon and dying only to become a butterfly.

4. Ask your child to make a butterfly as a symbol of Jesus' new life.

After Mass this weekend:

1. Talk about the day's scripture stories.

2. Share some ideas as to what your family can do to live out the Gospel message.

3. Talk about how the disciples had a hard time following Jesus. Share an example of how people today sometimes find it hard as well.

(Based on suggestions contained in the recommended guidelines of the Archdiocese of Cincinnati sacramental packets.)

CHRIST IS IN US

AS WE ARE IN HIM

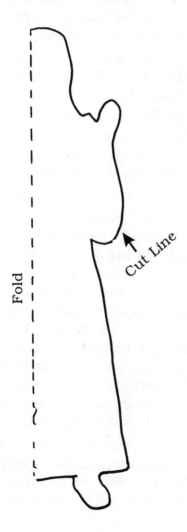

SESSION IV: The Party's Over – What Now?
A Love Feast Forever

Parents

7:00   Welcome and Prayer

7:15   Recap of previous sessions

This evening we come together to recap what we've learned about the eucharist and to move forward.

For most of us, the celebration looks different from what we remember about our First Communion.

Over the past few weeks we were reminded that the main concept of eucharist is the risen Christ among us and how we are to carry that into our own lives.

But what happened along the way was that the message got distorted.

We moved from focusing on the presence of Jesus in the Eucharist, in our lives and in our community to dwelling on the rules and regulations. We concentrated on fasting from midnight until after we received the host. We focused so much on rules that we thought that if we imitated Jesus suffering by obeying the rules we would be good enough. We forgot that Jesus loves us in spite of ourselves and that he asks us to live according to the Gospel.

Next we moved to a period of "magic." That the host and wine became flesh and blood. We concentrated so much on the transformation of the bread and wine that we forgot about the transforming power the eucharist has on us.

Then we moved to concentrating on a personal relationship with Jesus. People thought that the more times they received eucharist the better their place in heaven would be.

Some how the lack of understanding of Christ's presence moved us to focusing on the externals: the veils, the blue ties, arm bows, the pictures, etc.

What we have been challenged to do is to move forward by moving backward. Returning to the time of Jesus and what Jesus intended the eucharist to be. We are called to refocus on Christ's presence in the eucharist, in our community and in each one of us.

Perhaps, some of you would like to share one idea or something new that you heard that really spoke to you. (Allow time for comments.)

It is important to remember, that what we learned as children is not wrong, but it should only be a part of our understanding.

Re-creating our understanding of eucharist, doesn't happen overnight. We grow in the sacrament by regularly participating in the ritualistic celebration, by continuing to learn about our faith as adults, by sharing our faith with our families, each other and our community and above all through prayer.

Goal for this evening – an opportunity to get us in touch with our Sacramental Imagination

7:35   Video: *The Potter*

7:50   Guided Imagery using Romans 9:20-21

8:00   Small Group Reflection Divide into groups and discuss:

But who are you, my friend, to talk back to God?

A clay pot does not ask the man who made it, "Why did you make me like this?" After all, the potter who makes the pots has the right to use the clay as he wishes, and to make two pots from the same lump of clay, one for special occasions and the other for ordinary use.

Romans 9:20-21
Share your reaction to this scripture passage in light of understanding that our participation with the eucharist constantly reshapes and re-creates our life in Christ.

8:15   Join children for sharing and closing prayer. (You might wish to include light refreshments.)

8:30   Dismissal

Materials: Video: *The Potter* (Shepherd and Associates, 1978). Music and recorder, TV, VCR, video and tape, name tags.

Students

7:00	Students make name tags
7:05	Welcome and Introductions Opening Prayer
7:10	Icebreaker – M&Ms Directions: Have the children count off in groups of four (one group for each catechist). Leader invites students to take some M&Ms but to eat any yet. Tell the student that for each M&M they must tell one positive thing about themselves before they eat it. For example: "I got a good grade on my spelling test." "I helped with the dishes today." Note: It may be wise to have the students display their M&Ms first.
7:25	Music: Song of the Body of Christ Explain to the children that singing songs about Jesus is like praying twice. This is a very special song because it talks about how we share in the story of Jesus, how we are called to share the bread of Jesus with others. Remind them that we have been singing this song at each session but this time we are all going to learn the motions to the refrain. We will use this song as our closing prayer with our parents this evening.
7:30	Guided Imagery Directions: Quiet the children, Invite them to lay on the floor or put their heads down, close their eyes and concentrate on their breathing. Breathing out all their bad

thoughts or hurriedness. Breathing in all the goodness, all of God's love for them. Remind them that God loves them so much that he sent Jesus to be with us. Using children's scripture, a children's guided imagery book or in your own words, tell the story of Jesus, his friends and their last meal together.

After the story, remind the children that Jesus has invited them to that same meal. Talk about how they will feel. Ask them to think about how it will feel when the bread is given to them, when they receive the cup.

After a few moments say, "Breath in. Breath out." When you are finished, open your eyes, but continue to remain quiet. Look around and see those who are invited to come to the table with you.

7:45   Short Break

7:50   Activity – Chalice decorating
Directions: Talk to the children about the cup Jesus gave to his apostles. What did he say? What did he mean when he said, this is my blood, poured out for you? How can we share in that cup? How can we be cups for others? Tell the children that in a few short weeks, they will be receiving the cup of Jesus for the first time. What is in our cup to share with others? Distribute a "chalice" to each child. (You may use a simple shaped chalicecut out of heavy construction paper, a flat wooden one or a ceramic one). Have the children

decorate them with symbols, words or pictures of what their cup holds for other people.

8:15   Sharing – Parents join children
Directions: Invite children to share their chalice with their parent/s. Ask them to explain their design and why they included certain items. Allow 5 minutes.

8:25   Closing Prayer Directions: Ask parents and children to form two circles. The inside circle should be the children, facing outward. The parents should form a circle on the outside, facing their child.

Remind everyone, that throughout our times together we have been listening to a special song, "Song of the Body of Christ."

Tonight, the children are going to teach us the special motions that go with this song.

8:30   Dismissal (a special option, maybe to have light refreshments.

Materials: M&Ms, name tags, chalices, markers, music tape and boom box.

SESSION IV: Handouts

Homework

Family Reflection: Jesus Shows Us How to Celebrate Eucharist

During the week:

1. Read and reflect on Luke 24:13-35.

2. Tell your child the story of Jesus on the road to Emmaus.

3. Show the parallels of the Mass:
   Liturgy of the Word – Jesus' explanation
   Breaking of the Bread
   Christian Witness – sharing the message that Jesus is alive.

4. Ask your child to make a collage about the people who have celebrated the Eucharist as Jesus wants us to celebrate.
   Leave room to add pictures of family and friends who will be sharing in the celebration of your child's First Communion.

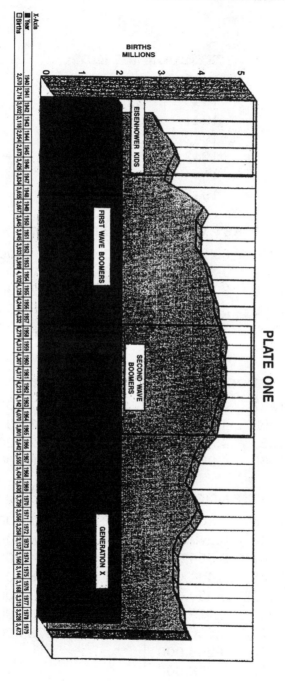

PLATE 2

PRE-BOOM (GI KIDS)

YEAR	BIRTHS
1940	2,570,000
1941	2,716,000
1942	3,002,000
1943	3,118,000
1944	2,954,000
1945	2,873,000

FIRST WAVE BABY BOOMERS

1946	3,426,000	1952	3,933,000
1947	,834,000	1953	3,989,000
1948	3,655,000	1954	4,102,000
1949	3,667,000	1955	4,128,000
1950	3,645,000	1956	4,244,000
1951	3,845,000		

SECOND WAVE BABY BOOMERS

1957	4,332,000	1961	4,317,000
1958	4,279,000	1962	4,213,000
1959	4,313,000	1963	4,142,000
1960	4,307,000	1964	4,070,000

GENERATION X (a.k.a. Baby Busters)

1965	3,801,000	1973	3,137,000
1966	3,642,000	1974	3,160,000
1967	3,555,000	1975	3,144,000
1968	3,434,000	1976	3,168,000
1969	3,630,000	1977	3,313,000
1970	3,739,000	1978	3,328,000
1971	3,556,000	1979	3,473,000
1972	3,258,000		
1972	3,258,000		

Plate 3 Sacramental Life of the Baby-Boom Generation							
(numbers in millions)*	1940	1950	1960	1970	1980	1990	2000	2010
Infant Baptism (under age 5)	10.6	16.4	20.3	17.1				
1st Reconciliation. 1st Eucharist, Confirmation (5-17)		30.9	44.2	52.5	46.0			
Formal Religion Vacation (1824)			16.1	24.7	29.5	25.2		
Return for Wedding and or Child's baptism (25-340			22.9	25.3	36.6	41.3	34.7	36.4
Boomer with Children preparing for 1st Sacraments (35-44)					25.7	36.6	41.1	34.5
Boomer's Midlife (Spiritual Midlie) (45-54)						25.3	35.6	23.2

Source: Current Populaton Reports, Series P-25, No. 704, "Projections of the Population of the United States: 1977 to 2050," U.S. Government Printing Office, Washington, D.C., 1977.

*National Conference of Catholic Bishops report that 25% of the U.S. population is Catholic.

Ontongeny of Ritualization						
Infancy	Mutality of Recognition					
Early Childhood		Discrimination of good and bad				
Play Age			Dramatic Elaboration			
School Age				Rules of Performance		
Adolescence					Solidarity of conviction	
Elements in Adult Rituals	Numinous	Judicial	Dramatic	Formal	Ideological	General Satisfaction

From Magic to Metaphor, 53.

Endnotes

Introduction

1. Summation of statistics by Wade Roof, *A Generation of Seekers* (San Fransisco: Harper, 1993) and Andrew Greeley, *The Catholic Myth* (New York: MacMillan, 1990).

2. While a significant number of parents in baptism classes are older baby boomlets (Generation Xers), averaging the ages of parents of children preparing for the sacraments of confirmation and eucharist with baptism, this percentage seems to ring true in other parishes as well.

Chapter 1

1. Various authors indicate between 76 to 77 million. For our purposes here, we will use the 76 million figure.

2. While similar baby booms were also noted in Australia and Canada during this time period, only the one which occurred in the United States was explored.

3. Kirk McNeill, "Reaching Out to the Baby Boomers," Continuing Ministerial Education Program, Cin-

cinnati, March 1993. His statements were substantiated by participants.

4. It should also be noted that even large percentages of Catholic women obtained birth control pills during this time period.

5. Based on research by McNeill and Roof as well as personal experience and research.6. Roof, 51.

7. Based on current trends in population growth, assuming an average of completed childbearing of 2.1 children per mother and deaths per year.

8. In reference to several new books which are being promoted on Baby Boomers, i.e. *A Generation of Seekers* and *A Culture of Disbelief* see bibliography for more information.

9. Notes from *Reaching Out to the Baby Boomers: A Workshop for Enhancing Evangelization,* facilitated by Kirk McNeill, March 1993.

10. Wade Roof, 35.

11. This is well noted in Robert N. Bellah, et al, *Habits of the Heart* (New York: Harper & Row, 1985) and *The Good Society* (New York: First Vintage Books, ed. 1992).

12. Roof, 41.

13. Kirk McNeill, *Going For the Baby Boomers –* Workbook (Nashville, MFG Publishing, 1990), 7.

14. Bellah, 144.

15. "Baby Boomers Have Created Their Own Religious Shock Wave," *PRRC Emerging Trends,* Feb. 1994:16.

16. Roof, 26-30.

17. Wade Clark Roof, "The Four Spiritual Styles of Baby Boomers," USA Weekend, (March 19-21, 1993), 4.

18. Roof, *Generation of Seekers,* 26-30.

19. Greeley, 32.

20. A number of books have been written recently about the need to evangelize those already in the pews. Patrick Brennan's books noted in the bibliography are helpful here.

21. Roof, 176.

22. Champlin, 5-7.

23. Interesting note: Roof, 176, shows 11% are no longer Catholic, 7% are non-religious, 4% are other faiths and 31% are Catholic but inactive.

24. Despite many parishes' attempts to emphasize "sacramental readiness" age/grade level are still the most prevelant guidelines used.

25. The sacraments of initiation are typically the "drawing cards." Reconciliation is a sacrament many parents state that they dismissed long ago as having little to relevance in their lives; however many Returnees hold that this sacrament is their reentry to Church.

26. Greeley, quoting James Joyce, 47.

Chapter 2

1. Brennan Hill, *Rediscovering the Sacraments* (New York: Sadlier, 1982), 7.

2. Greg Dues. *Catholic Customs and Traditions,* (Mystic: Twenty-Third Publications, revised 1992), 150.

3. George S. Worgul, *From Magic to Metaphor* (New York: Paulist Press, 1980), 43.

4. William J. Whalen. *How Different Christian Churches Celebrate the Sacraments* (Clarian Publications, 1980), 5.

5. Worgul, 123.

6. *Ibid.*

7. Greeley, 44.

8. In his book, *The Catholic Myth*, Greeley states that the sacramental imagination is the view of the whole world as sacrament. In the many interviews I conducted not one person mentioned the idea of the world as sacrament. But they did identify with a sacramental imagination that connects the ritualistic action with the essence of Christ.

9. Alex Garcia-Rivera, "Sacraments: enter the world of God's imagination," *U.S. Catholic* (Jan. 1994: 6-12), 6.

10. *Ibid.*

11. Garcia-Rivera, 12.

12. Worgul, 41.

13. *Ibid*, 49-59.

14. As the reader can see by reading the first section, no other generation has lived so fully in "age of crisis" as the Baby Boomers. For a clearer understanding of the Baby Boomer's sociosis, Baby Boomer Blues by Collins and Clinton is a valuable resource.

15. One may find further enlightenment in reading *Habits of the Heart*.

16. Worgul. 5.

17. *Ibid*, 3.

18. *Ibid*, 223. Worgul's work identifies what my research illuminates.

19. Brennan Hill notes.

20. In reference to the Beatles. This attitude was prevalent in the 60s, and by its very definition seemed to relate to the Beatles song.

Chapter 3

1. Hill, Brennan, various discussions and presentations, 1993-96.

2. Worgul, 226-228.

3. *Ibid*, 7.

4. *Ibid*,16.

5. A smaller, but significant percentage of adults showing up are preboomer, "Eisenhower kids." They are the grandparents who have now assumed the responsibility for their divorced children's children. There is also a slim number of Generation Xers. Most of these are confined to Baptismal Preparation.

6. It is important to recall that Boomers do not have a good relationship with either authority or institutions, often holding them in contempt. For many the role of the priest has been diminished; however, "Father says" still contains significant power.

7. Greeley, 49.

8. *Ibid*, footnote, 165.

9. Joseph Champlin, *The Marginal Catholic* (Notre Dame: Ave Maria Press, 1989), summation of premise.

10. Hill and Madges, 54.

11. Robert Bellah, et al. *The Good Society* (New York: First Vintage Books, 1992), 158.

12. Worgul, 7.

13. *Ibid*, 78.

14. Greeley, 13.

Chapter 4

1. Greeley, 13.
2. Marge Blessing, Archdiocese of Cincinnati.
3. Patrick J. Brennan, *Re-Imagining the Parish* (New York: Crossroads, 1993), 115.
4. *Ibid*, 70.
5. *Ibid*, 110.
6. *Ibid*.
7. Champlin, 105.
8. Greeley, 232.
9. "A period of stagnation: the waters are muddied, and a sluggish disorder prevails. The inferior (mud) is on the rise, the superior (clarity) on the decline. In such times, the wise man takes shelter in his own integrity, and looks deeply within until the outer waters clear." Andrew Welch, Oracle, 1992.
10. Champlin, summation of theme.

Chapter 5

1. Many similar programs exist throughout the United States. The one I used as a foundation was the Lorretto Project from the Diocese of Worchester, Massachusetts.
2. I left the parish in the middle of the second year, before further developments and implementations occurred.